JIMMY WILDE

(1892

UNDISPUTED CHAMPION OF THE WORLD FROM 1916 TO 1922

The Mighty Atom ↘

The Tylorstown Terror ↘

The Ghost with the Hammer in his hand

D. BEN REES

JIMMY WILDE (1892–1969) THE UNDISPUTED FLYWEIGHT CHAMPION OF THE WORLD FROM 1916 TO 1922

ALSO KNOWN AS: THE MIGHTY ATOM, THE TYLORSTOWN TERROR AND THE GHOST WITH THE HAMMER IN HIS HAND

D. BEN REES

Pont-y-gwaith

Pontypridd

Written by D. Ben Rees

This book is presented to the memory of Gilbert Odd: editor, boxing correspondent and the one who encouraged the author to appreciate the world of Jimmy Wilde

Designed by WorkBook Press of Las Vegas, Nevada

ISBN:
PB: 978-1-957618-20-3
ebook: 978-1-957618-21-0

Tylorstown

CONTENTS

Chapter 1

IN PRAISE OF JIMMY WILDE

As a boxing enthusiast, I remember vividly how men in my home village in west Wales would talk often of the incredible talent that flourished in the Rhondda valleys in the first three decades of the twentieth century. Jimmy Wilde, Percy Jones and Tommy Farr were always mentioned, with the experts agreeing Jimmy Wilde was one of the greatest fighting men to ever come out of Wales – a boxer who made an impact not only in the valley towns but in England, and particularly so in Liverpool and London. Before the end of his brilliant boxing career, he also travelled to fight in the home of boxing, the United States of America.

In his 1990 book *Welsh Warriors*, Fred Deakin posed the question 'Who is the greatest fighter who ever lived?' and admitted there was no one answer. We each have our own idol, our hero, and, while the question might be valid to an historian of the ring, Deakin is right. To me, Jimmy Wilde was a sensation, and the various names bestowed upon him tell a story. The best known of those names must be the Tylorstown Terror and the Mighty Atom; however, Pedlar Palmer, the English boxer who held the world bantamweight title from 1895 to 1899, was inspired to call him the Ghost with a Hammer in his Hand. These terms show how Wilde's contemporaries viewed the hard-punching flyweight champion of champions.

He fought as a flyweight and never at any time throughout his career came close to scaling the limit for his class. Whenever he had to weigh in for a contest at eight stone, Wilde rarely had to remove his overcoat, while his opponents often had a difficult task in keeping within the limit.

Fighting in the flyweight division was something of a hindrance. Then, as now, it was the heavyweights who got the most publicity and drew the biggest crowds. Jack Dempsey could draw 120,000 fans to watch him box the Frenchman Georges Carpentier in New Jersey. A flyweight was lucky to have two thousand spectators, with the exception of Jimmy Wilde. He became a sensation, for he broke the mould. In the second decade of the twentieth century, boxing was thrilled with such a flyweight. Wilde was, without doubt, the most amazing boxer of his generation, and the sports writers competed with each other in their description of his style, coverage, skill, power and love of boxing. Their nicknames included Tetrarch of the Ring, Mauling Miner, Human Hairpin, Jimmy the Great Killer and Welsh Wizard as well as those already mentioned.

At one period in his boxing career, Wilde weighed under seven stone. Even wearing the heaviest overcoat, he could find in Pont-y-gwaith or Tylorstown, he was well below the flyweight limit of eight stones. This wasn't necessarily a hindrance; little Jimmy enjoyed his food and could eat as much as he wanted, even when training and preparing for a big fight. On the day of the fight, he never had to stress about being too heavy for his class.

Nonetheless, this little miner could deliver a blow any featherweight champion or lightweight champion would have been proud to possess. Wilde had acquired the ability to place the whole of his meagre bodyweight behind his deliveries. He also hit with the knuckle part of his gloves so that almost every punch of his would land on his opponent with destructive power or, at the very least, score another point to be rewarded in the referee's book.

Some boxing historians have called Jimmy Wilde a freak, and one cannot disagree. His skin-and-bone physique was a distinct disadvantage for a Rhondda pugilist who combined his apprenticeship in the boxing booths with the demanding work of cutting coal in a local colliery. Yet Wilde's advantage, even then, was his almost uncanny skill of being able to avoid the blows of his adversary.

The diminutive Welshman seemed to display a sixth sense in his ability to avoid an oncoming punch by moving his head a split second before impact. He was also able to duck and swerve to minimise the effect of a blow to the body. Nine times out of ten, he would avoid the blow altogether, until some of the distressing fights at the end of his superb career.

Naturally, being exceptionally light, Jimmy Wilde was extremely fast and the majority of the boxers he defeated over his long career were dazzled by his speed and dexterity. Too often, his style caught them completely off stride, meaning Wilde was able to dispose of them before they had time to plan a counterattack.

In fact, Wilde's counterpunching was truly deadly. Few boxers in south Wales or elsewhere were able to retaliate so swiftly and so accurately after making an opponent miss punch after punch. This happened all the time when Jimmy was in his prime. His Welsh fans followed him to London or New York, marvelling at how their hero, with his wisp-like torso and pipe-stem arms and legs, produced those devastating punches. Yet careful scrutiny of his physique disclosed a pair of shoulders which would have done credit to a man several stones heavier than him. His back was bunched with muscles, developed from hard labour in the mine.

As a boy, Jimmy had gone to work with his father in the local pit for half a crown a day. His small size meant he could crawl into the narrow seams, where he picked away at the coalface. The short, vicious strokes he used were driven from his back and shoulder muscles. It was this back-breaking and heavy work in Tylorstown that ultimately made the young Jimmy strong and resilient and in possession of a powerful punch. His extra muscular build and natural talent made him one of the outstanding fighters during the First World War.

Chapter 2

CHILDHOOD

It is odd how hardly anyone who has written on Jimmy Wilde knows where he was born. Biographers seem to have mixed up Quakers Yard near Edwardsville and Treharris with Pontygwaith, close to Tylorstown. In fact, Quakers Yard and Pontygwaith are twenty miles apart. Quakers Yard is located in the Taff valley, while Pont-y-gwaith is found in the Rhondda Fach valley.

Even Jimmy Wilde himself got at least some of it it wrong in his book *Fighting was My Business*, originally published in 1938. This is what he writes:

> I suppose my birthplace, Number 8 Station Road, Pont-y-gwaith (Craig Berthlwyd, Quakers Yard) next door to, and really part of Tylorstown, was in no way different from the hundreds of other cottages lined up all exactly alike to look at, all covered with the grime of the Rhondda Valley.

In fact, William James Wilde was born on 12 May 1892 in Craig Berthlwyd, Quakers Yard, near Treharris which is a long way from Tylorstown. His father, James Wilde, worked in one of the pits of the area, presumably as a miner (though I have no evidence to back this). When Jimmy was a year old, his father and mother Maggie (born Margaret Anne Hughes, the daughter of a miner) moved to 8 Station Road, Pontygwaith, which is located on the boundary with Tylorstown in the Rhondda Fach.

During the mid-1870s, new collieries were attracting people to the area. There was a lot of migration to Rhondda Fawr (the larger valley stretching from Porth to Treherbert) and Rhondda Fach, from west Wales in particular. Men arrived to work in the new pits at Ferndale and Tylorstown, bringing their families with them.

It was David Davis (1797–1866), the owner of steam coal collieries at Blaengwawr near Aberdare and Abercwmboi in the Cynon valley, who leased the mineral rights to 500 acres of land in Blaenllechau. He encountered numerous difficulties, including transporting machinery over the mountain from his base in the Cynon valley. A reference to these problems can be found in a Welsh-language poem published in 1880:

> *Heb heol yn unman, na dim ond ceffylau*
> *I gludo yr ymborth a'r gêr at y gwaith.*
> (Without a road anywhere and only horses / To carry the food and machinery to the workplace.)

His son, also called David Davis, and elder brother of Lewis Davis, came to the rescue, and advised his father to sink to a much greater depth in order to access the steam coal seams. On 14 June 1862, the Four Feet seam was struck, and the Davis family subsequently grew rich. The industrial era of the Rhondda Fach had begun. A colliery was opened in Pont-y-gwaith, but it remained idle for years until it was reopened and renamed Ferndale No. 8 Pit instead of Hen Bwll Waynes, Pont-y-gwaith.

It was an Englishman, Alfred Tylor of Newgate Street, London, who opened the second large colliery concern in the Rhondda Fach. Sinking began in 1873 but, due to geological difficulties, it was several years before coal was dispatched to the docks in Cardiff.

Tylor was distinctive in the sense that all the other coal owners of the two Rhondda valleys were staunch Welsh-speaking speculators, like Mordecai Jones and James Thomas. Tylorstown was named after him.

The exploitation of the coal resources of the Rhondda Fach valley continued from 1862 to 1884. By then, six different companies were operating nine collieries and production was a staggering million tons of coal. The face of the countryside had been completely transformed by terraced housing, an urban ribbon in the Rhondda Fach stretching from Ynys-hir to Maerdy at the top of the valley. In 1890, four years before Jimmy Wilde was born, the collieries of the Rhondda Fach were controlled by a few companies: Locket's Merthyr, David Davis and Sons, Alfred Tylor, London and South Wales (Wattstown) and Ynys-hir Steam Coal.

The Rhondda valleys became home for the Wilde family. The houses comprised five small rooms and were built for between £120 and £140. Rent ranged from four to five shillings per property. Local Rhondda historian Dr E. D. Lewis describes the dwellings on Station Road, Pont-y-gwaith, and similar houses as follows:

> These houses were built of drab, local pennant sandstone and massed in long, parallel, monotonous streets, crowding the valley bottom or extending in terraces along the mountain slopes. Little garden space was provided and, of course, there were no bathrooms, despite the fact that nearly all the occupiers were miners.

It is interesting that Jimmy's earliest memory was his father arriving at Station Road from the colliery and washing himself in the tub in front of the fire. Years later, Jimmy wrote in the first chapter of his autobiography of the daily occasion:

> It was not only a ritual of cleanliness – up to a point – but it also coincided with meal-time and in those days, I was ready to eat. Few of the children of the mining families in Tylorstown were over-nourished, and there were times, particularly during the strikes, when starvation was not far away.

Jimmy would be sitting in the living room cum kitchen which housed the whole family when his father returned after a hard day's toil. Black-faced, indeed black all over, his father's first task was to take off his coat and shirt. Next, he would attack the coal dust on his face, arms, neck and chest. Once he had put on a clean shirt, the family was ready to eat together. Everything depended on the shift he was on: if it were a night one, they would sit down for breakfast, or if it were a day shift, they ate supper together. Once a week, on a Friday, the Wilde family witnessed a dramatic change in James Wilde. With huge effort and help from his wife and Jimmy's older sister, James' back was washed until it was as white as the rest of his muscular body. It was a ritual throughout the Rhondda and was another additional strain on his mother, who had a great deal of pride in her frugal, poverty stricken home.

As soon as he could walk, Jimmy was out in the street. It was his playground, for only carts and horses were to be seen in the roads of Pont-y-gwaith. By the time he reached his sixth birthday, he was fending for himself against other children from Station Road, who took advantage of the fact he was so small and thin. From then on, Jimmy was always ready for a fight, leading to his neighbours regarding him as a born troublemaker. The Welsh Nonconformists, with their numerous chapels, were growing in strength in Tylorstown and the Rhondda Fach and they were united in their opposition to boxing. These Pont-y-gwaith residents frowned on the fact that Jimmy was always in trouble, and had been able to hurt his contemporaries.

Jimmy admits in his memoirs that he was a pain to others. So stunted and undernourished was he that he was subject to constant verbal insults. Although he was easy prey for local bullies, he instinctively wanted to protect his pride and was growing up with a huge love for boxing. Jimmy was fair game for those looking for trouble, but he always fought back and was willing to stand up to the bullies even when they were much stronger and bigger than him.

Jimmy was never out of some kind of trouble, but he often escaped being mauled or caned. 'There was not enough of me to hit squarely,' he said, 'and I proved adept at dodging weighty blows or kicks and getting in with a lot of quick punches myself.' Even in those early days, from the age of seven to ten, it seemed clear Wilde would one day find himself in a boxing ring.

During Jimmy Wilde's boyhood, the Welsh mining industry was in a crisis. The miners' leader was the local Member of Parliament William Abraham (1842–1922), better known by his Welsh bardic name of Mabon. Abraham was adored by the miners, Jimmy's family included, for he tried his utmost to avoid strikes in the mining industry. In 1893, the hauliers' strike was devastating in its consequences, and Jimmy's family suffered the same fate as most of the other families in the Rhondda valleys. The 1893 and 1898 strikes brought 8 Station Road, Pont-y-gwaith, to the very depths of poverty. Despite being children, Jimmy and his sister would go 'coal poaching' – literally fetching coal from the tips and selling it on for a few pence in order to help their parents financially. Jimmy has provided a graphic account of what it entailed for him and his obliging sister.

The children had to start from home before five o'clock in the morning and tramp across uneven terrain for some five miles from Station Road to the location where the coal was stacked. They had little time to fill their own sacks and stagger back with the heavy weight on their shoulders. Undoubtedly, both children were in a state of collapse by the time they arrived at Pont-y-gwaith and, to reach school on time, they would stash the coal in a secret spot. After school, they visited elderly people, widows in particular, who were grateful for the coal they sold for a reasonable price.

Jimmy had little time for school and hated every minute of it. He longed for the freedom to pursue his own activities, carrying sacks of coal and fighting all comers. Hard work, insufficient food and bad diet, and a meagre education were his lot as a young child.

At the tender age of thirteen, he decided to follow in his father's footsteps and become a miner. His was the same path followed by James Griffiths, a future politician from west Wales, and Aneurin Bevan, founder of the National Health Service in 1948. Like Jimmy, both men became miners when they were thirteen years old. His salary in 1905 was two shillings daily. Wilde had his eyes opened, for the atmosphere in the collieries was extremely religious. Like Mabon for example, the men began their shift with prayer. Outside the collieries, chapels were overflowing due to the Welsh Revival of 1904–05. The main leader of the religious movement was Evan Roberts of Loughor in west Glamorganshire, a young theological student who had been a miner himself for thirteen years. One of Roberts' lieutenants was the Reverend D. M. Phillips at the Presbyterian Church of Wales, Libanus Chapel, Tylorstown. A powerful figure in Tylorstown for decades, Reverend Phillips also taught adults. Jimmy Wilde came to respect this man, who looked like an Old Testament prophet with his dark beard and ready stock of Calvinistic doctrine.

By a strange coincidence, the diminutive Welsh lad decided not to accept a job in Ferndale or Tylorstown or Pont-y-gwaith. Instead, he chose the Treharris Colliery, near his birthplace in Quakers Yard and the deepest coal mine in the world in 1905. It was initially a wise choice, but after a few months, Jimmy returned to his beloved Rhondda Fach.

Chapter 3

UNDER THE SPELL OF THE 'MOUNTAIN FIGHTER'

Jimmy Wilde had two strokes of luck as a young boy-helper at the colliery. First, he found himself in the same shift as Dai Davies, a well-known boxer in east Glamorganshire (who was to become Jimmy's future father-in-law); and second, owing to his incredibly small size, he was employed as a worker on the coalface. This did not generally happen to boys as young as him. They were usually given the job of looking after the doors that the trams of coal came through – a hazardous enough job, but not in the same league as being on the coalface. It was this early work which was responsible for his abnormal shoulder development.

Dai Davies was a great character and belonged to those pugilists known in south Wales as 'mountain fighters'. He participated in secret, illegal battles in the Welsh countryside around Penrhys and Maerdy, and across the wider Rhondda area. These were grim battles which were always fought without gloves, and which lasted thirty or forty rounds, or sometimes until one of the boxers was knocked unconscious. Often, Dai and his fellow 'mountain fighters' would tramp over difficult terrain for at least ten to twelve miles before they came to the agreed spot. The location would be unknown to the police and the spectators would follow them there. Then, these brave warriors, foolish though they might have seemed to their religious contemporaries, would face one another and box ferociously. Blood often flowed from their noses and cheeks; their faces were pounded out of all recognition. And their reward? A few measly pounds collected among the onlookers or a side stake put up in a public house.

They fought at dawn in these isolated, out-of-the-way places, mostly during the summer months. The Welsh poet William Williams (perhaps better known by his bardic name of Myfyr Wyn) recollects how the bleak mountains between Tredegar and Rhymney were saturated with blood on Mabon's Day, the first Monday of the month after payday. This one-day holiday was the result of an agreement between the coalmine owners and the unions, and was enjoyed by many across south Wales during the last decade of the nineteenth century. On Mabon's Day, some dozen 'mountain fighters' stripped to the waist and fought each other until they could no longer stand.

Dai Davies had a number of contemporaries in the Rhondda Fach who were always ready to step into the ring. The most well-known of these 'mountain fighters' were Evan Roberts and John Richards from Maerdy, in the upper reaches of the Rhondda Fach. In 1885, they decided to fight each other on the Merthyr mountain, well away from Maerdy. Their hard-fought battle lasted over an hour and a quarter. In *Wales and its Boxers: The Fighting Tradition,* Professor Gareth Williams describes the struggle thus:

> Richards possessed of only one eye, and his opponent, alive to the advantage to be gained by placing the solitary organ hors de combat, devoted all his energies toward that end.

Williams also mentions two Rhondda miners, Hutchins and Northey, who were ever ready to battle it out on the mountains of Glamorganshire. These two hard men had been bound over by the Bridgend magistrates to keep the peace:

> At Cockett, a district within the town of Swansea, the police were deceived when their followers divided into two, and they eventually exhibited their art and sullen craft at Cwmdonkin Park, where Northey was banged so fiercely around his eyes and nose that he failed to come up to scratch for the fifth round.

Northey survived, unlike many of the 'mountain fighters' who were killed on the mountain side. There is a long list of those brave but mad mountain fighters who lost their lives for nothing, leaving their wives in dire financial straits and their children fatherless. Professor Williams' book provides the evidence, names and the verdict on their illegal activities.

Cornelius Collins was a giant among the 'mountain fighters', as Dai Davies well knew. In 1890, he fought John Hughes, a hardliving haulier in a Rhondda colliery, on Llanwynno mountain, near the mining village of Ynys-y-bŵl. Collins gave Hughes a rough ride, with the haulier ending up in a coma. He never recovered and died of his injuries. A manslaughter charge was brought against Collins.

In May 1894, Twm Edwards, a mountain fighter from Aberaman, near Aberdare, faced his opponent in a converted slaughterhouse. Edwards was a brother of a Labour Party pioneer, Councillor Wil Jon Edwards, who wrote a classic autobiography, *From the Valley I Came* (1956). Twm Edwards and David Rees were fighting for a prize of twenty pounds. Their encounter was civilised, for at least they wore five-ounce gloves. David Rees did not die from a punch but the way he fell to the floor and hit his head. Twm Edwards was charged with manslaughter and spent some time in prison.

Dai Davies taught the young Jimmy all the tricks at his command: how to hit your opponent hard, how to develop your footwork and evade the punches, and how to preserve one's stamina and strength.

Their association came about when Jimmy was working with Davies as his 'boy'. Jimmy remembers seeing Dai one day with his face battered and his knuckles raw. He smiled when Jimmy asked him what he had been doing, answering:

> Just keeping fit, boy, just keeping fit.' Jimmy

> persisted in his questioning.

'Well, if you must know,' said Dai Davies, 'I was fighting'. His blue eyes twinkled with pride.

'How long did it last?' Jimmy asked.

Dai answered, 'Oh, thirty-nine rounds, and I will admit I wasn't sorry my man did not feel like it anymore'.

With boxing his passion, Jimmy could not believe he was working with such a hero and immediately put Dai on a pedestal.

Dai was a huge person, and Jimmy learned a great deal from him. His wife was a staunch chapel-goer in a thriving Nonconformist chapel, who strongly disapproved of any form of fighting, legal or illegal. Dai also had a daughter, who was some two years younger than Jimmy.

Jimmy has described vividly his experience of working with Dai:

> Being small, I could easily get in low stalls where the bigger men found it hard. I would sometimes be able to start a tram, thus letting Dai work harder, and getting the tram raced more quickly. To race a tram meant to fill it, putting a wall of big lumps of coal round the side, and making a 'wall'; the smaller stuff went inside, so that it would not fall off. No matter how hard the seam, nor what difficulties (stood) in the way, six of those trams had to be filled by two men – or a man and a boy – before they earned a full week's wage.

Jimmy loved every minute he spent in the company of Dai Davies, especially when his mentor was in a good mood. Over tea and sandwiches, Dai would remember some of the hard-fought fights on the mountain side. One of his most notable bouts was against Ted 'Chops' Williams. The two veteran mountain fighters slogged it out for eighty-four rounds in a fight lasting several hours. Dai eventually won on a knockout blow.

It was soon after talking about his exploits with Jimmy that Dai questioned the younger man's passion for the ring, asking him: 'Tell me, Jimmy, is it true you have ideas about serious fighting yourself?'

The lad was hacking away at a seam and covered with coal dust when he answered, 'It is so, Dai, but with my weight, what can I do?'

Dai was not going to accept excuses, however, and he replied: 'That's true. Your feet are as important as your hands, Jimmy, as I've told you often enough. One day, I will see you fight. We might be able to make something of you!'

'You really think I could?' Jimmy asked.

Dai chose his words carefully. 'Didn't your hero Freddie Welsh begin in much the same way? And is he much bigger or heavier than you?'

Jimmy idolised Frederick Hall Thomas, known as Freddie Welsh. Despite being six years older than Jimmy, the two men became sporting contemporaries and made Welsh boxers very welcome in the boxing rings of America.

Dai's comparison hit home. Later, Jimmy recalled:

To be compared with Freddie Welsh, men in that vague fashion, gave me a joy that I had not experienced before. Dreams began to make a cleaner shape. If Welsh had succeeded against the obstacles of weight, height and the mines, why shouldn't I? I longed for the day to come when I would be able to show Dai what I could do, and a bond of friendship was forged between us.

Jimmy heeded Dai's advice, his teaching and the tactics he thought were needed. It was Dai who gave him his first and only boxing lessons in a tiny bedroom. Jimmy wanted desperately to earn a few extra shillings in the boxing booths that visited Tylorstown and other Rhondda towns. His father was ailing, and colliery work demanded healthy miners. Jimmy also realised there was a great deal of tension between his parents. He knew they were unhappy and it concerned him. His words, written years later, sum up the situation:

> Looking back, it is hard to blame either of them. Only the physically fit were really pulling their weight in the home or down the pit, terms which were really synonymous. And father was a long way from that.

Jimmy had a valid reason for earning extra money – to ease the financial stresses of his parents.

Dai Davies was just the man Jimmy needed at this time of his life: a seasoned fighter of the old school. Dai could help the young miner to realise his dreams and took Jimmy under his wing. He invited him to come to his home for some initial coaching and taught him the fundamental rules of the game, polishing up any weaknesses in Wilde's repertoire of moves and ambitions. Jimmy has given us an excellent account of the 'bedroom bouts' as he calls them:

> The room, like all those in Tylorstown cottages, was tiny, and even when the bed was pushed against the wall and the other furniture placed on top of it, there was all too little space. But Dai pointed out the less space to move in, the more important the quick footwork and bodywork. He showed me how a move of an inch or even less could make all the difference to the power of a blow given or received.

Each session lasted at least an hour; however, they had to practise quietly, so as not to disturb Mrs. Davies who had no time for such a violent sport.

The bedroom was an ideal spot in which to practise, for there was hardly any space in which to move at all. Jimmy's footwork and body swerves were of utmost importance and it was in the small confinement of the totally inadequate 'gymnasium' that he picked up the amazing ring craft and fighting strategy that was to carry him to the championship of the world.

Jimmy longed for a proper ring, but he could not find what he was looking for. So instead, he arranged a 'mountain fight' at a street end with lads who were three or four stone heavier than him. Dai would hear of these fights on the grapevine but his life was full and busy. He could spare very little time on Jimmy outside those bedroom practice sessions.

Then, one day, Dai saw Jimmy in action. His opponent was Tommy Davies, who weighed nine stone, for Jimmy was under six stones. They fought a few rounds before Tommy lost his temper and came out of his corner like a wild animal. Jimmy stood his ground, his feet planted a foot and a half apart. As Tommy came in with his defence wide open, Jimmy landed him with his right fist. It connected perfectly. Tommy staggered backwards, only to collapse on the ground and be counted out. Dai Davies' training sessions had taught him what he called 'ring craft'.

Dai Davies was pleased at what he'd witnessed and was determined this fifteen-year-old lad should be introduced to the world of the boxing booths. He had served his apprenticeship and was now ready to confront opponents like Tommy Davies as well as higher calibre fighters.

Chapter 4

THE REVIVAL AND JIMMY'S ACCIDENT

As Jimmy Wilde prepared for more boxing matches, he was surrounded by those who regarded the game as violent and cruel. In 1905, boxing was not regarded as the best sporting event for young people. When he became friendly with Dai Davies' daughter, Elizabeth, he discovered she resented his passion, and her father's own fights, especially when he ended up badly beaten.

Nonconformists, who were strong in the Rhondda Fach, began to criticise boxing in the local press and in their monthly gatherings. Progressive attacks on boxing were not confined to Britain. There was similar condemnation in the United States of America, where a journalist wrote that the 'art of self-defence' was the 'most useless of all arts' because there was no longer a need to defend oneself with fists. By 1905, the American reformers, as well as Welsh-orientated social gospellers, believed they were on the threshold of destroying boxing altogether.

However, there were other views. Writing in Britain, E. B. Osborn wrote in the journal *The Nineteenth Century* that 'the lad who learns to box invariably becomes a law-abiding person, and, if he must fight, will always fight like a gentleman'.

What worried the middle-class reformers was not the sport of boxing as much as the money paid out to the two men who fought each other. President Theodore Roosevelt, who met Jimmy Wilde's Member of Parliament William Abraham (Mabon) in 1905, wrote: 'When money comes in at the gate, sport flies out through the window'. Mabon himself was a devout chapelgoer and he as a Lib-

Lab did not object to boxing matches as he would attend a few in his home area in the upper reaches of the Rhondda Fawr. It bothered him as a successful politician that those who ran the successful boxing events in London would exploit working class men. Those who were behind boxing a sport were not people that Mabon mixed with but he felt a close affinity to the career of Jimmy Wilde and wished him well He was concerned, as were the Rhondda chapel women, that those fighters, who were sometimes beaten mercilessly, often had to retire without any finance or insurance or cash to care for them. Sometimes they were badly injured or even killed.

Roosevelt saw corruption lurking in the corner of every ring. He wrote:

> The money prizes fought for are enormous, and are a potential source of demoralization in themselves, while they are often so arranged as either to put a premium on crookedness or else to reward as amply the man who fails as the man who succeeds.

In fact, Theodore Roosevelt did not like to reward the losers. It offended his sense of justice.

In Wales, the 1904–05 religious revival brought an entirely new interest to young people who were in the mainstream of chapel life or who were attracted by its emotional appeal. The revival was a remarkable example of popular religion. It originated from the people, those living in mining valleys and rural villages, whose emotions and religious attitudes helped shape it. These people consciously repudiated the ministerial guidance on other attempts to guide and control it along past and traditional lines. As a result, the leadership of many chapels passed into the hands of young people.

In fact, the revival reversed the roles of members of the congregation. Before it started, the task of arranging the chapel's affairs and conducting its meetings was in the hands of the minister and the diaconate. Women like Mrs. Dai Davies were the most numerous attendees at the meetings, but the task of addressing those meetings on relevant topics was exclusively the work of the men present. Miners also got involved, though there is no evidence Jimmy Wilde was one of them. The revival saw young people taking over these meetings and women like Mrs. Davies and her daughter (whom Jimmy had taken a fancy to) becoming more prominent.

The revival through the main evangelist Evan Roberts had made a huge impact on sport. Rugby clubs ceased to exist and public houses emptied. Innkeepers stopped working for the breweries and attended the chapels, and hardened drunkards became elders and ministers. The strong-willed Seth Joshua who had great interest in boxing before the revival became a Welsh Presbyterian evangelist under the movement known as the 'Forward Movement', a home missionary movement which founded chapels in the Rhondda. The revival only lasted eighteen months and boxing never declined as much as other sporting events but Jimmy Wilde was not untouched by its emotionalism as the revival became a significant episode in the life of every South Wales colliery and in particular in the Rhondda. In his autobiography Jimmy wrote in his autobiography on Evan Roberts.

To make It more difficult, Evan Roberts, the famous evangelist who always travelled with his three sisters was in Tylorstown, attracting hundreds to his tents, weeping, wailing, frenzied with religious fanaticism; and if I had a semblance of a black eye people would go to the other side of the road to avoid me. Fighting was made a deadly sin by Evan Roberts!

Around this time, an accident happened which nearly wrecked Jimmy's chances of a boxing career. He was promoted to work at the pit head, where his job was to check the trams as they rolled from the pit head to the sidings, and to oil the pulleys. The accident happened without warning. Jimmy was alone, oiling the sheaves of the pulleys, which were in constant action as they hauled ten coal-laden trams the two-mile distance. While he worked, the rope swung around and knocked him off his feet. Jimmy later wrote of the experience:

> Before I knew what had happened, I was lying on the ground with the fast-moving rope going over me. I lay horrified, too frightened at first to shout. When the journey stopped, some mile away from where I was lying, I managed to crawl away.

It was a brave act on Jimmy's behalf, for the rope had carved a deep hole into the back of his calf, close to his ankle. He managed to crawl slowly away, but by now he was shouting. With blood pouring from the wound, he collapsed. It wasn't until an hour later that Jimmy was discovered and the colliery doctor, Dr. Morris, attended him.

Jimmy realised there was a strong possibility his leg would have to be amputated and he implored the doctor to save his leg. Dr. Morris promised to do his best, dressed the wound regularly, and provided Jimmy with the crutches he needed for a few months.

Life was a struggle. His sick pay was inadequate, so Jimmy depended on the community spirit of neighbours, relatives and fellow miners, particularly his mentor Dai Davies and family.

He had plenty of time on his hands, so he began to read everything he could on boxing. Books were borrowed from the Mining Institute and newspapers were given to him by those who knew of his ambition. When he was able to hobble there, he would spend hours on end at the Tylorstown Library, reading current boxing news in *The Rhondda Leader, Cardiff Times* and many other newspapers. He had fallen under the spell of Freddie Welsh, and he looked forward to the boxer coming to Ferndale and Tylorstown for exhibition bouts, so he could go and watch him carefully. Jimmy was amazed at the speed of Freddie Welsh and how he could be so hard-hitting.

During his recovery, Jimmy frequently visited his 'second home', Dai Davies' house, where he saw a great deal of Dai's daughter Elizabeth (Jimmy generally called her 'Lisabeth'). Under the care of Dr Morris, he regained his strength and confidence, and, within six months, he was free of pain and the wound had healed, leaving him with just a blue mark, nearly two inches in diameter. Friends doubted he would ever be able to stand up in a ring for twelve to fifteen rounds, but Jimmy proved them wrong. Now, he was ready to begin his apprenticeship in earnest.

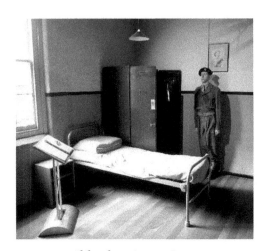

Aldershot Army Camp

Arthur Frederick Bettinson

Boxing Ring

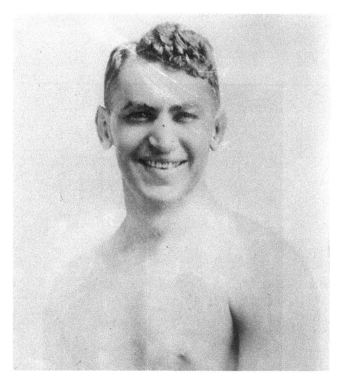

Battling Levinsky

Jack Johnson

Matt Wells

Pancho Villa

Tommy Farr

Joe Louis

David Lloyd George

Chapter 5

LIFE AT THE BOXING BOOTH

Jimmy was so determined to follow his great ambition that he got involved in the world of boxing booths. Boxing booths were a travelling circus whose performers were up-and-coming boxers. Some of the best ring men Britain had produced had themselves graduated from the boxing booths.

Let me explain what it involved. Spectators were invited to stand up in front of the skill and punching ability of the booth's boxer during a stipulated number of rounds. The reward for the successful person who stood on his feet for three or four rounds ranged from £1 to £5. The challenger only got his money when he was successful, which was rarely.

The most attractive part of every circus was the booth. This was a temporary structure and usually erected as people entered the arena. The ring itself was small and known as a 'rat trap'. The boxer was obliged to take on all challengers and to entertain the crowd with his ability to duck out of danger. It was not unusual for a boxer to fight sixteen different men in the course of a single evening. By the early 1900s, the boxing booths had become less common in circuses and travelling fairs but were still a common sight in the valleys of Wales. One of the best-known boxing booths was in Aberdare, a few miles over the mountain from Tylorstown, and was run by Jack Scarrott. It was in that booth that Jimmy fought for five years. Scarrott offered a pound to anyone who could last three rounds with this pale-looking 'human scarecrow', as he was described by one spectator. Jimmy would usually take on fifteen men, all of them bigger and heavier than himself, in one evening.

It was no easy living, no rose-strewn path from Tylorstown to Aberdare and back again. Even so, Jimmy was on top of the world. He was easily beating all comers, who fell like ninepins. None challenged his aspirations of fistic fame.

The irony was that many of the sightseers, miners like himself but with no particular boxing skills, were attracted to the boxing booth because they anticipated getting the better of tiny little Jimmy. He at least could be encountered without any great danger of being beaten, they reasoned.

Many of these challengers must have had the surprise of their lives, for not only did they find it practically impossible to land a lumbering blow on the wisp-like figure in front of them, but when Wilde stepped in and cracked one of his dynamic punches to the chin, they were usually snuffed out like a candle. No wonder he became known as 'the Ghost with the Hammer in his Hand' in the boxing booths.

By now, the family desperately needed money. His father had fallen ill and his earnings decreased. Jimmy had no choice but to trudge along to the boxing booth in the evenings after he had finished his shift in the colliery. But soon everything changed. Scarrott arrived in Tylorstown, and the proprietor staged an eight stone six pounds' competition. in his home community. Although he only scaled six stone eight pounds, Wilde entered the competition, and knocked out his two opponents in a pair of rounds apiece, beating the other finalist in four rounds to win the competition and a coffee set.

Gareth Williams reminds us of another occasion when Wilde knocked out seventeen opponents in a morning, and after a relaxing lunch of a bun and a cup of tea, knocked out another three in the afternoon. The total sum of money handed to him came to only thirty shillings, but that was a lot of money to Jimmy – nearly as much as he earned underground as a miner for a whole week of hard labour. The famous referee, Ike Powell, whose brothers Abe and Jack were Wilde's contemporaries in the same booth, remembered Jimmy knocking out every one of his twenty-two opponents one Bank Holiday Monday in Swansea.

Then Jimmy decided to buy a house in Tylorstown and get married to Elizabeth Davies on thirty-five shillings a week – a step that nearly robbed the boxing game of one of its most famous personalities.

For Elizabeth, as an evangelical Calvinist chapel-goer, objected to boxing, and Jimmy had to abandon his fistic ambitions before she would accept him as her husband. Elizabeth had one failing though – a love of chocolate almonds. Jimmy began to buy her plenty of them. It eventually cost the price of chocolate almonds – money earned in the ring – to buy her off and help her as she agreed to take in Jimmy's mother after the death of his father, three younger siblings as well as to recover another sister from care. This explanation of how young Jimmy continued with his boxing career is the one given by him to us in his autobiography. The choclate almonds did the trick to overcome Elizabeth disapproval of boxing. It seems to be a very unusual, unothrodox way of convincing a person who had been for years anti-boxing to become pro boxing. I do not expect many to be convinced by his kind deeds The couple would go on to have two sons of their own. As the family breadwinner, Jimmy had little choice but to maintain two jobs.

Booth life was hard and so was mining. Yet Wilde's tiny frame was sufficiently strong to enable him to do a hard shift in the colliery, followed by another in the 'rat trap'. His success in the boxing booths eventually led to him leaving the colliery to tour with the booth for two months. Wilde was expected to take on all challenges. To encourage opponents to come forward, Jack Scarrott would offer £1 to anyone who could stand up to Jimmy for three rounds. It was hugely effective publicity, but unfortunately it meant he became the central attraction, taking on most of the booth's challengers.

On one memorable occasion, Jimmy fought no fewer than sixteen fights. In fifteen of them, he knocked out his opponent inside the stipulated three rounds; however, the last opponent, who was 5ft 10½ inches and scaled near the lightweight poundage, somehow managed to stay the full course and earned his pound.

Fame travels with the wind, and it was not long before those in the legitimate boxing business got to hear about the sensational Jimmy Wilde at the Scarrott boxing booths in Aberdare, Tylorstown, Tonypandy and Swansea. Promoters at small towns where the booth might have visited were anxious to have him star on their bills, and the little lad found this a much more profitable and less arduous way of earning a pound or so. He began to apply for these contests himself, but his small stature was a decided drawback. Jimmy was told on more than one occasion that he looked as if he was suffering from consumption and should not be boxing at all. He was in a dire situation.

Eventually, Ted Lewis, a south Wales boxing manager, came to hear of Jimmy. Ted asked Jim Driscoll if he would accompany him to see 'a little boy' he thought might turn out to be a good boxer. By now, the 'little boy' was approaching his twenty-first birthday. Driscoll had been brought up in the world of the boxing booth and, at that time, was the acknowledged boxing oracle in Wales. He obliged Ted Lewis and together they went to a charity show in Pontypridd to watch Jimmy take on George Dando.

Talking about his experience, Jim Driscoll later said:

> It was the first time I had seen Wilde. He was a mere speck of a fighter weighing not more than six stones and had conceded his rival about a stone-and-a-half and received ten bob for his efforts. The bout was only a few rounds and judging by the frailness of this boy, it was enough. He lost on points that time, and

my opinion of him as a fighter was that he was a game one, but had plenty to learn. I told Lewis what I thought of him, and concluded by saying that I didn't think he would go far as a professional at that weight, mainly because there wasn't a championship for lads of so small a poundage. And as I couldn't see him gaining much weight, I thought he was wasting his time.

Well, that was Jim Driscoll's first impression of a lad who was to be an even better boxer than he ever achieved himself in an outstanding career. Teddy Lewis was the one who saw greatness in Jimmy and he recognised some spark in him that Peerless Jim had obviously missed. He interviewed the Tylorstown scrapper and was intrigued to discover his age and the fact he was married and had a great deal of family commitment. Teddy Lewis was so taken with his frankness, honesty and self-confidence that he immediately undertook there and then to see what he could do for him. This was Boxing Day 1910.

Jimmy could finally turn his back on the years he had spent in the boxing booth. According to James Butler, a boxing writer of distinction, Jimmy Wilde had fought 864 fights of which he only lost four. Jimmy had joined Peerless Jim and Owen Moran as someone who had learnt his craft in the tough world of the boxing booth. During his career, Wilde defeated Pedlar Palmer, Frankie Neil, Pinky Evans and Digger Stanley, to name but a few of the many to have graduated through the world of the boxing booth.

CHAPTER 6

MAKING A NAME FOR HIMSELF

Under Ted Lewis' management, Jimmy became a semi-professional; however, he remained a miner for a few years more. In fact, his last pay sheet at the formidable No. 8 pit owned by D. Davis & Sons Ltd was on 1 April 1913, when he was earning £67- 9 for a fortnight's work. One shilling was deducted to pay the salary of the check weigher of the colliery and 1-7d for the services of the colliery doctor, leaving him with £6-5-2. No wonder Jimmy left the mining world for boxing. At least they would pay well if he succeeded in his bouts.

Boxing, according to Joe Palmer, the famous referee, 'is a showman's business, when all is said and done'. In his interesting autobiography Recollections of a Referee, published in London in 1927, he claimed that five boxers had elevated boxing into a complete new realm as a spectacle, namely Bombardier Billy Wells, Derek Smith, Jimmy Wilde, Ted 'Kid' Lewis and Johnny Basham, a native of Newport.

Wilde never viewed himself in his early years as a professional boxer, or throughout his career as an extraordinary individual, and he never behaved in a manner that made people talk and laugh behind his back. The American Jack Johnson was very different – he sipped beer and vintage wines through a straw; he laughed loudly, rolling his head backwards as he did so into an almost ninety-degree angle. He was so egocentric that he employed a maid to look after his clothes. Jimmy Wilde possessed only a few suits, while Johnson had twenty of them.

Johnson would change his clothes three times a day! Wilde never forgot the fact that he was a miner, and when he left mining altogether, he felt guilty as he admitted in these words:

> But I was extremely self-conscious when I visited the homes of working miners; after all, I was something of a pariah, earning a living with my fists. Yet there was never a suggestion of reproach, and it was easy to slip into an acceptance of the fact that I was a full-time professional fighter.

Boxing, like music, is a rhythm sport, and a unique activity. The exercises Jimmy did with Ted Lewis at Pontypridd's Millfield Athletic Club day after day – jumping rope, punching the special bag, shadow boxing with his sparring partner and doing sit-ups – were in essence rhythmic movements. Every great fighter has his own rhythm and style; Wilde danced around the ring, making his bouts a pleasure and delight to witness.

As Wilde boxed, he lived for the game of boxing. It was this more than anything else which won over his wife and converted her into an enthusiastic fan. When Jimmy fought in Pontypridd, Elizabeth was there at the ringside, the chapel girl who'd once uttered 'Amen' at religious meetings now calling out 'Come on, Jim.'

Hers was a complete turnabout, which began when she walked with Jimmy to the boxing booths. During a rail strike, the couple walked for miles over the mountains to Caerphilly, where Scarrott had a busy booth, Elizabeth carrying her youngest child. Jimmy tried his best to persuade her to stay at home, but she was a determined fan.

When Ted Lewis arranged for Jimmy to fight Young George Dando, a hard-hitting pugilist from Merthyr Tydfil, first in Pontypridd and later at other venues, everyone knew he had a difficult task ahead of him. Jimmy had never indulged in the gambling and heavy drinking that were a constant temptation to boxers; the chapel-reared Elizabeth would not have allowed it. In fact, one must commend the zeal of Elizabeth; while she annoyed Ted, she was not a person to be fobbed off easily. She was familiar with the anti-boxing views of her mother and the proboxing views of her father. She was Dai Davies' best friend, and the best friend Jimmy ever had. Elizabeth brought him family comfort and had experienced a huge conversion in her outlook towards boxing.

Ted Lewis arranged before the end of 1910, for Jimmy to fight Les Williams at Pontypridd. The fight lasted three rounds. Jimmy wrote of the experience, '[I was] vaguely aware of the thunderous applause when the miners had realised I was not only lasting a round, but going to win.'

The following year saw Jimmy fight at least twice a month at Pontypridd. On New Year's Day, his opponent was Ted Roberts; he knocked him out in three rounds. Roberts must have been a glutton for punishment because he stepped into the ring against Jimmy for a second time on 25 May, when he was knocked out in two rounds.

Jimmy fought 28 bouts in 1911, 27 of them in Cardiff and Pontypridd, and one in Edinburgh. Every month, he travelled to Pontypridd, sometimes after a shift at the colliery. The boxers he faced in the ring were local talent and long forgotten, the details of their lives yet to be recorded by a boxing historian. Few were able to last the stipulated rounds. The boxing bouts were held in the spacious upstairs room at Pontypridd's Welsh Harp Hotel and Jimmy would often walk here from Tylorstown.

On 10 January, he fought Dick Jenkins, who lost on points after a six-round bout. Ten days later, Jimmy was back to take on Dai Davies also known as Dai Chips. Dai was a local lad, and he gave Jimmy plenty to think about. He admitted Dai was the most difficult fighter he had met during his early semi-professional career.

In February, Jimmy had two contests. On the second night of the month, he fought against Kid Pearson and knocked him out in round two of a six-round contest. On 10 February, he faced George Lake, and, like Dai Davies, Lake lasted well. Indeed, the verdict was a draw. In March, there were two contests. Jimmy fought Dick Jenkins in Cardiff on the ninth and Jimmy won on points. On 20 March, he returned to the Welsh Harp to beat Dai Thomas with a technical knockout in the third round.

April was a busy month for the Tylorstown miner. He fought three times in Pontypridd. On 4 April, he fought against Archie Grant; on 10 April, he fought against Eddie Thomas; and on 20 April, he took on Billy Papke. They were all knocked out: Grant in round three, Thomas in round two and Billy Papke in round three.

Jimmy was on top form, as his opponents found out in the month of May. On 5 May, he met Dai Roberts who was no match for him, knocked out as he was in round three. It was the same result against Archie Grant on 15 May, and Ted Roberts on 25 May.

On 3 June at the Welsh Harp, Billy Brown was on the floor in the fourth round, and failed to beat the bell, while 20 June saw Fred 'Kid' Morris giving Jimmy a hard-fought but worthwhile contest. Wilde won by points over six rounds. In July, Jimmy fought once at the Welsh Harp, this time against Steve Thomas, whom he knocked out in three rounds. He made up for this quiet month in August with three contests, two of which were in Pontypridd and one in Scotland in Edinburgh. On 8 August, he won on points against Fred Chappel, and on 26 August, Dick Jenkins took him to the eleventh round. In that round, the referee awarded Jimmy a technical knockout. Both contests at the Welsh Harp were watched by Elizabeth, Ted Lewis and Jimmy's boisterous Rhondda Fach fans.

Ted arranged for his protégé to travel outside Wales for the first time in his life, to meet Jim Easton in Edinburgh. Before the fight, Jimmy frightened the life out of his trainer. After a long train journey from Tylorstown to Edinburgh, he signed in at the hotel and decided to have some rest on the comfortable king size bed. A few minutes later, he was sleeping without any concern for the important fight. Jimmy awoke to loud banging on his bedroom door. The door opened, and Ted Lewis and David Hughes rushed into the bedroom.

'What on earth is it?' asked Jimmy.

'Is the man crazy?' cried Ted in anguish. 'You're due to fight in twenty minutes.'

It proved a fight. he would never forget. Jimmy lasted and boxed well against a difficult boxer. He won on points over ten rounds. Ted Lewis was pleased. It was a step nearer to being accepted by the London-based promoters. They came back to Wales well pleased with themselves, forgetting all about the sleeping episode and concentrating on the victory.

In September, Jimmy was on top form. His trip to Edinburgh had given him a great deal of confidence. On 9 September, he knocked out Young Avent in round four, and then on 20 September (at the same venue in Pontypridd) he did the same with Ted Powell, this time in round three.

In October, Jimmy, under Ted Lewis' guidance, went into the ring on three occasions. He knocked Joe Rogers out on 10 October in five rounds, while on 20 October, Young Powell only lasted three rounds. In November, he met with real success, which pleased his supporters, the fellow miners. Welsh miners were keen boxing enthusiasts, and the south Wales coalfield has supplied a large number of skilled boxers like Percy Jones of Porth. On 11 November, Wilde knocked out Young Powell in round three, and Young Rice on 20 November in four rounds.

In December, Young Powell volunteered to meet Jimmy Wilde again. He had been badly beaten on 11 November, but was back for more of the same medicine almost exactly a month later on 12 December!

It was the same story next time around: Powell was knocked out in the first contest in three rounds, and it was the same in the second contest. Ted Rogers was his opponent on 20 December, and he was knocked out in round four, while Young Jennings did much better – he lasted the twelve rounds. Jimmy Wilde won on points. It had been a successful year. The future looked bright for him, and Elizabeth and the boys. His small stature still worried the promoters when they saw him in the flesh; but once he was in the ring, they were always glad, convinced and very supportive.

CHAPTER 7

FIGHTING WAS HIS PASSION

Jimmy Wilde made a huge step forward at the beginning of 1912 when Ted Lewis managed to arrange for him to meet Matt Wells' Nipper at The Ring, Blackfriars Road, Southwark, on 20 January. Pale-skinned and with a child-like innocence in his guileless grey eyes, Wilde was almost prevented from fighting Matt Wells' Nipper. The Ring promoter Dick Burge feared being accused of child abuse if he allowed the poor miner from the Welsh valleys to be slaughtered in front of the Cockneys of Blackfriars.

Matthew 'Matt' Wells (1886-1953) had taken part in the Olympics held in London in 1908 in the lightweight division and this meant that Jimmy was much lighter than him. He lost to Frederick Grace, who went on to win the Olympic Gold Medal. The following year, Wells turned professional and, in 1911, he defeated the excellent Freddie Welsh in a twenty-round bout to win the lightweight championship of Great Britain. He took home the Lonsdale Belt, and was the first Jewish boxer to be bestowed with such a boxing honour. The win gave him the European Boxing Union lightweight championship.

Wilde stood his ground with the promoter Dick Burge, pointing out he was already a husband and a father, and a fully consenting adult! He pleaded for an opportunity to show his skills and, after a long conversation, Burge gave the go-ahead. Given his opportunity, Jimmy proved to Burge and the Cockneys that he was no pushover and knocked out his opponent in one round.

One Cockney shouted out to Wells, 'Hey, Nipper, don't swallow the leek in one mouthful!'

The year 1912 proved to be a year of successes, as Wilde won one contest after another. He travelled to Liverpool Stadium in Pudsey Street, Liverpool, on 1 February to meet Young Baker, a local lad with huge potential, and won comfortably. For the next two fights, his opponent was Sam Jennings, who, at the beginning of his professional career, was known as Young Jennings. He lived in the Welsh-speaking village of Dowlais, some two miles to the north-east of Merthyr Tydfil. Jennings fought occasionally between 1910 and 1918, but his career was not a particularly busy one. He had nine bouts and some 91 rounds, and two of these bouts were in 1912 against Jimmy Wilde. They met on 15 February 1912 at Millfield Athletic Club in Pontypridd, and three weeks later at the Badminton Club in Cardiff. Jimmy won both bouts easily, though on points over six rounds. He had no matches during the month of March, but he was expected to meet Roland Hall in Cardiff on 4 April. Wilde was on top form, making certain Hall could not carry on after the fourth round. Ted Lewis allowed him the rest of April, May and June without any boxing commitments, so that he could work and spend time with his loving family in Tylorstown.

The next important contest was on 20 July at the Welsh National Athletic Club in Cardiff against Fred 'Kid' Morris, who lived in St George's, London. This was not the first time they had met. He had fought Jimmy in Pontypridd on 20 June 1911 and lost on points over six rounds. On the second occasion, the contest had been arranged over twenty rounds but Morris was glad when the referee stopped the contest in the fifth round. Fred 'Kid' Morris was no match for the miner from the Rhondda. He had fought Billy Padden twice and Jimmy Wilde twice in a very inactive career. He had only six bouts during his career; he lost four of them and drew two, never winning a single contest. He should have never been foolish enough to agree to a contest with Jimmy.

On 3 August 1911, Jimmy Wilde appeared for the first time at the Pavilion, Tonypandy, in front of his loyal fans. His opponent this time was Joe Gans, a Baltimore boxer living in Wales, and he had no hope of gaining a victory over the 'Mighty Atom'. Gans was a fixture at Tonypandy with the promoter Scarrott using him as often as he could throughout 1911 and 1912. He lost seven of these contests in Tonypandy in 1912. He made another debut against the 'Mighty Atom' on 3 August 1912 and he was easily beaten in the seventh round of an eight-round contest. The verdict? A technical knockout in favour of the Rhondda Fach hero. On 17 August, Jim Suckey was the opponent against Wilde, again in Tonypandy. In the eighth round, Wilde won by a technical knockout.

In September, Ted Lewis, Jimmy and Elizabeth travelled to Sheffield to Attercliffe Boxing Hall, where he fought Walter Hall. Hall was no match for Jimmy, for he could barely stand in his corner by the third round of a six-round contest. The referee gave Jimmy a technical knockout verdict. They enjoyed an evening in a hotel in Sheffield after the contest before leaving the following morning for Wales. Ted Lewis looked upon Jimmy as his own son and in Sheffield he told the boxer the month of October would be free from any contests, but November would be different for he had lined up for him a number of interesting encounters.

On 9 November, at the Olympia Rink, Merthyr, Jimmy fought the Welsh flyweight Phil Davies. He won in the second round with the referee having to intervene to save Davies from further punishment. On 13 November, he was at Swansea to meet a boxer from Aberdare. Llewelyn Boswell began his boxing career on 4 March 1910 at the Athletic Club, Swansea, against Joe John, and won on points. Boswell loved to fight in Swansea, especially at the Sporting and Athletic Club. The fight against Jimmy Wilde was the tenth of his career. Boswell did well against a polished pugilist and lost on points over six rounds.

Three days later, Jimmy was back at Scarrott's Pavilion in Tonypandy, this time up against Jim Ransford in a twenty-round contest. Ransford was not even up to the standard of Boswell, and it did not astonish the boxing reporters that he had to retire in the second round. On 23 November, Jimmy travelled to the Pavilion in Mountain Ash in the heart of the Cynon valley to meet Kid Pearson, who lived in Openshaw in Lancashire. Kid Pearson had had a dismal boxing record since he began his career in 1904. He had lost every contest, except the one against Young Cleary on 5 January 1905 at the Labour Hall, Manchester. He lost to Tom Stafford in Winslow, Herbert Gratton in Mansfield and Young Challas in Manchester. On 23 November, in his first ever fight in the valleys of Wales, Kid Pearson lasted just two rounds against the Mighty Atom. The referee decided to call it a day for the Lancastrian and Pearson retired gracefully, waving goodbye to swollen eyes and lips forever.

On 30 November 1912, Jimmy Wilde travelled to Pentre in the Rhondda, the home of the famous Welsh politician and trade unionist William Abraham (Mabon). Mabon was proud of Jimmy's mining roots, as he was the leader of the powerful South Wales Miners' Union, of which Jimmy, his father and father-in-law were loyal members. In turn, they admired Mabon and his way of keeping the miners in work, avoiding at all times a strike which could bring the miners into poverty. Mabon came to see Wilde box at his hometown of Pentre. Alf Williams, Jimmy's opponent, hailed originally from Merthyr Tydfil and had moved to the mining village of Treherbert. He made his debut as a boxer on 11 May 1908. Alf Williams survived the fifteen rounds and lost on points. Out-boxed in front of family and friends, he decided he'd had enough. After the defeat, he hung up his gloves and retired. He could see he would never have the ability Jimmy Wilde possessed.

Wilde's next fight, on 14 December 1912, was at the Pavilion, Tonypandy, against Stoker Staines of HMS Indomitable. Staines was no match for him, and he could not last three minutes in the ring with the future world champion. Staines was knocked out in the first round of a fifteen-round contest. This gave Wilde more confidence to travel to the Theatre Royal in Cardiff after his Christmas celebrations with his family. On 29 December, Jimmy met Billy Yates from Bargoed, in the Rhymney valley. The Cardiff referee made Yates retire in the fourth round of a fifteen-round contest.

Jimmy had an extremely heavy schedule leading up to the end of the year. He would have liked to spend Christmas Day and New Year's Day with his family; however, he was facing two difficult contests. The first, on 28 December, was at the Marquee, Tonypandy, and Jimmy's opponent was a Rhondda boxer, W. Stuckey of Llwynypïa. Jimmy won easily again over six rounds. His next fight involved a long journey, for on 30 December he was facing Glaswegian P. J. Billy Padden at Victoria Hall, Glasgow. The referee was Brummy Meadows, and Wilde weighed in at six stone eleven pounds, while Padden was six stone thirteen pounds. It was unusual for Jimmy to have an opponent who was nearly the same weight as him. The Scots were entertained to superb boxing by both men. Padden was Wilde's best opponent of the year. Jimmy won on points over twenty hard-fought rounds.

In 1912 and 1913, there was a great deal of discussion as to the possibility of Jimmy Wilde fighting more often in London, and perhaps travelling to the United States of America. Ted Lewis discussed a proposed tour more than once with Charles Harry, who knew the American boxing scene well. He had an arrangement for a large number of British boxers to travel to New York and other boxing centres. There was one obstacle: despite his impressive number of winning bouts, Jimmy was simply not heavy enough. The Americans love heavyweights more than any other weight.

The two Rhondda boxers who were chosen to travel to the USA were Les Williams of Tonypandy and Dai Bowen of Treherbert. They were not in the same league as Jimmy Wilde, but they fitted the bill as far as Charles Harry was concerned. They left for New York on the Titanic, and were among the hundreds of people who lost their lives in that dreadful disaster when the ship ran into an iceberg. Had Jimmy gained a few extra pounds, there is no doubt he would have shared the fate of his two friends. He tried hard to convince Harry to let him go and he was forever grateful to providence that Harry hadn't relented.

Jimmy took a leading part in the huge gymkhana at the Athletic Grounds, Tonypandy, held in memory of the two promising boxers and to raise money for their families. The event was under the presidency of L. W. Llewelyn. Thousands attended the gymkhana, competing in the muscular competitions, tent pegging, lemon-slicing and fencing; however, it was boxing, the passion of the Rhondda valleys, that was the main attraction.

The organisers succeeded in attracting the best Welsh boxers of 1912. The main attraction was Jimmy Driscoll, then featherweight champion of the world, followed closely by Jimmy Wilde. Then came Lewis Williams and William Phillips, both of Pen-y-graig, Dai Matthews of Trealaw, F. Davies of Ferndale and Harry Davies, Maesteg, who was middleweight champion of Wales. Jack Phillips, Jack Jones and Sam Owen from Aberaman in the Cynon valley attended, as did E. W. Davies and Jimmy Rees of Porth. Then there was Kid Evans of Trehafod, Bandy Davies from Pontypridd, as well as Young Beddoe and Young Midgets from Pentre. Jack Harrison, middleweight champion of England attended, as did Digger Stanley, bantamweight champion of the world, and Eddie Morgan, a prospective bantamweight of great talent. All these men came together willingly, driven by their belief in the brotherhood of boxers. Many had made a huge effort to join Driscoll and Wilde. The boxing fraternity was joined by scores of artists, baritones, and comedians such as Dai Hooper from Treherbert, Jack Granfield from Treorchy and Jack Twissell of Tonypandy. Bands were in attendance:

The Swansea River Minstrels, Tonypandy Hibernian Bands, Cory Workmen's Band and the Llwynypïa Drum and Fife Band.

Ted Lewis asked Jimmy Driscoll to second Wilde in some of his forthcoming fights. The request was the catalyst for a deep and wonderful friendship between the two boxers. Driscoll seconded Jimmy when he fought Young Jennings, at one time the world flyweight champion, and Wilde won easily over eleven fierce rounds. Jennings made generous remarks: 'Very good, very good, Jimmy! Keep it up. He even said that Jimmy was on his way to become another star like Sam Langford. Langford was one of Wilde's heroes. He knew about boxing if anyone did.

CHAPTER 8

THE VALLEY BOXER

The presence of Jim Driscoll in Wilde's boxing career was important, for Jimmy Wilde had never received any formal instruction. At once, Driscoll noticed a marked improvement in Wilde's abilities and found that, apart from Wilde's natural gift for fighting, he possessed an alert brain which enabled him to grasp the finer points of self-defence without needing to be told or shown twice. Jimmy picked up ring craft so rapidly that by 1913 he had been transformed into a boxer of world-beating class.

The ambition of Ted Lewis and Jimmy was to fight within the sacred precincts of the famous National Sporting Club (NSC). Members of the Club (as it was known) came from England's elite: the Earl of Lonsdale sat on its board of governors and Sir William Eden, father of Anthony Eden, who became Prime Minister after Winston Churchill in the 1950s, was a well-known patron. By 1913, Ted Lewis felt Wilde had served his apprenticeship in the boxing booths and venues of south Wales, as well as many an industrial town in the north of England.

When he first heard about the Welsh miner, Arthur 'Peggy' Bettison, the astute club manager of the National Sporting Club, shook his head and would not be persuaded into giving Wilde a chance. 'I have enough trouble on my hands, without asking for it,' he said, echoing the response of Dick Burge at the Blackfriars ring. Fortunately, Dan Sullivan, his matchmaker, was looking for an opponent for a young and promising boxer named Matt Wells' Nipper. Sullivan smuggled Wilde into the dressing-room of Rowland Hill's one-time

Nonconformist chapel, and then hid himself while the diminutive Welshman walked out to the ring to meet the Nipper. The fight was billed to last ten rounds, but as we have mentioned before, Wells didn't get further than the first round.

Jimmy Wilde had made a sensational London debut, but it did not get him the contests at the National Sporting Club he so eagerly sought. Mr Bettison, in spite of the crushing of Matt Wells' Nipper, still set his face sternly against allowing, in his opinion, a 'freak' to perform at the NSC of all places, and Jimmy had to face 1913 without a London appearance.

It was back to Tonypandy in the heart of Rhondda valley and nearby Swansea, another Welsh boxing town. Jimmy's first fight of 1913 was against Tommy Hughes of Blackburn on 18 January. Hughes made a valiant effort, but was no match for Wilde. He retired in the seventh round of a fifteen-round contest. Referee Ralph Lile stepped in to save Hughes from further punishment.

On 1 February, at the New Marquee, Tonypandy, Jimmy met local boxer Dick Jenkins from Cilfynydd, near Pontypridd. Jenkins did well and survived the ten rounds, only to lose on points. On 15 February, Young Fitzpatrick came to Tonypandy from Birmingham. Though he had an excellent reputation he only lasted three rounds.

On 8 March, Dai Matthews of Porth was the opponent. Jimmy and Dai were great friends, and Dai did well, for he often acted as a sparring partner for Jimmy. This time his friend had to retire. Jimmy and his team travelled to Swansea to meet local boxer Harry Taylor on 31 March. Taylor retired in the third round against the unrelenting style of Jimmy.

Jimmy had returned to Tonypandy by 12 April to meet Will Rees of Mountain Ash. Rees was knocked out in the second round. A week later, Jimmy was again in Tonypandy – this time fighting against Billy Yates of Bargoed. He won in the fourth round. Both Rees and Yates were heavier than him, with Rees two stone heavier than Jimmy. On 24 May, Jimmy met a boxer who hailed from Tylorstown. During that decade, Tylorstown had a number of excellent boxers, and Dai Davies was one of them. He gave Jimmy a hard fight, but his fellow townsman easily gained victory by points. That night, Tonypandy's Skating Ring was alive with excitement for Dai 'Chips' Davies and the Tylorstown Terror. The fans were divided in their allegiance, though they all knew that Jimmy could not be beaten by 'Chips', or anyone else from the mining valleys of Glamorganshire.

On 14 June, Jimmy fought the well-matched Glaswegian Billy Padden at Tonypandy. It was a hard-fought contest, and he won by points in a twelve-round contest. The contest was for twelve three-minute rounds for a side stake of £25,000 and the promoter's purse. It went the distance, though Padden was knocked down several times, and the referee gave the victory to Wilde on points. The following Saturday, Jimmy fought at the then new Boxing Marquee at Tonypandy against Gwilym Thomas of Pontycymer. It was a contest of fifteen two-minute rounds, and Thomas had a huge advantage weight-wise, being a stone and a half heavier than the Mighty Atom. It was Wilde, however, who possessed the better boxing skills. The referee stopped the fight in the fifth round, and Wilde was awarded the contest. His fellow Tylorstown boxers were equally successful that night. W. Fry won in two rounds against John Evans from Porth, while Dai 'Chips' Davies defeated Llew Morgan. Charlie Yeomans from Pontypridd drew with Harry Stuckey of Llwynypïa.

Within a few days, Jimmy was back in the ring, this time at the Pavilion in Pontypridd, where he met Dick Lewis of Aberaman. After only three rounds, in which hard blows were exchanged, Lewis, a brave pugilist, gave in. Charlie Yeoman was his next opponent and Wilde was declared the winner once again.

On 19 July, Jimmy again faced his great boxing friend George Dando at the Pavilion, Tonypandy. Wilde won the fifteen-round contest on points. He had been fighting regularly in Tonypandy since 12 April, attracting large crowds, the biggest being at Wilde's defeat of the former seven-stone champion of the world Billy Padden.

On 4 August, Jimmy fought Darkey Saunders of Camberwell in Cardiff and won on points. At the end of the month, he travelled to Liverpool to one of the strongest centres of the boxing game in the country, which had witnessed some of the finest contests this side of the Atlantic. Boxing was started in the Pudsey Street Stadium in 1911 by Arnold Wilson, who later became one of Britain's leading promoters. In 1911, the place was known as the Gilbert Hall, and had been used as a skating rink. Jimmy Wilde was a favourite with the Liverpool crowd, and his boxing skills were on display on 28 August as he fought against a local lad from St Helen's, Jack Dyer. Dyer survived three rounds of a fifteen-round contest, before the referee had to stop the fight to spare him more punishment.

Back in Tylorstown, Alf Harry, proprietor of the Assault-at-Arms in nearby Ferndale, had arranged a contest between Jimmy and Dicky Jenkins of Cilfynydd, a mining village near Pontypridd, on 6 September. They had fought previously and Wilde was facing a man at least a stone heavier than him. The contest went the full distance, though Wilde was the easy winner on points. Alf Harry presented Jimmy with a massive silver cup and also a purse of gold. Referee Harry Warne, himself a boxer, came all the way from London, as he had such esteem for Jimmy, and he was soon going to box for Alf Harry. On 8 September, a contest was fought between Dai Miles of Tylorstown and Harry Warne. Warne was a born gentleman, evidenced by him giving all the prize money to Miles. Jimmy Wilde was the referee. It was not his first time. In fact, his first experience appears to have been in August 1912, when Evan Evans ('Pom-Pom') of Pen-y-graig was called upon to defend the title of the middleweight championship of the Rhondda in Tonypandy against Billy Rosser of Porth. It was a fifteen-round contest, and it was obvious Evans was a tired man, having fought three times in a month. He lost the contest, his one and only defeat. The other contest Wilde had refereed was between two more Rhondda boxers, Mike Flynn of Clydach Vale and Mick Coleville of Treherbert. Jimmy called a draw. In both contests, his refereeing skills impressed the boxing fans.

Jimmy had a heavy schedule ahead of him after the Ferndale contests. On 9 September, he travelled to Drill Hall, Sheffield, for an evening fight with Dido Gains from Vauxhall, London. It was a hard-fought contest, and Wilde won on points after fifteen rounds.

He remained in London, where, on 11 September, he faced Harry Curley of Lambeth at the Olympia Skating Rink, Hanley. Curley was badly beaten and retired in the twelfth round. Wilde had endeared himself to the boxing fans of the Potteries, and the miners of the Staffordshire coalfield, who were his greatest supporters. He remained in the Stoke-on-Trent area to meet another London boxer, Kid Levine of Aldersgate. Levine was saved by the referee in the seventh round of a fifteen-round contest.

Between these fights in England, Jimmy returned to Wales to fight George Dando in Cardiff on 22 September. After their July contest, Dando fought in a masterful way; however, Wilde again won on points over a twenty-round contest.

On 1 November, he again met Darkey Saunders of Camberwell, this time at the Pavilion Skating Ring in Tonypandy. The referee stopped the fight in the eleventh round of a fifteen-round contest. Jimmy was back at Pudsey Street Stadium, Liverpool, for 13 November, and his opponent was a local Scouser, Young Baker. The referee decided Baker should retire in the tenth round of a fifteen-round contest. A week later, on 21 November, Jimmy met Jack Dyer of St Helen's at Manchester. They had met earlier on 28 August. This time, Dyer had given up on his chances by the second round, and

Jimmy had to travel immediately by train from

Lime Street to the Drill Hall, Swansea, to meet an exceptionally fine boxer called Dido Gains, of Vauxhall in London. Dido Gains was a clever and powerful boxer, as Jimmy knew from having met him a year earlier in Sheffield. However, even when Gains was apparently carrying everything before him, his head would be rocked back by Wilde's right glove popping up from nowhere to land under Dido's chin. Wilde had boxed and won in two rounds at Manchester during the previous evening, and had travelled two consecutive nights as well. The referee Frank Bradley, one of the best in south Wales, was amazed when he heard of his exploits. This time, Dido kept him for the whole fifteen rounds. Wilde won on points, and received a huge applause from the two thousand boxing fans at the Drill Hall.

On 2 December, in Tonypandy, he met another London boxer he had fought a few months earlier, Jack 'Kid' Levine, this time knocking him out in round twelve. Ted Lewis had arranged four more contests for him before the end of 1913. On 6 December in Merthyr, Wilde won on points over a ten-round contest against Young Dando, and on 13 December, he was back at the Pavilion, Tonypandy, facing Billy Charles from Bargoed. This time, the promoter was Ralph Lile, and Jimmy gained another victory when Charles retired in the sixth round.

Jimmy and his team travelled to Manchester Free Hall on 15 December for a fight against Harry Brooks of Aldersgate. Brooks was highly regarded by London promoters, but he was no match for the Tylorstown boxer. The referee intervened during the ninth round to save Brooks from further punishment. Lile arranged another bout for Jimmy at Tonypandy on Christmas Eve against Kid Levine This time, Jimmy knocked him out in the eighth round.

1913 had been a busy and rewarding year. Jimmy Wilde had won every contest, and yet the London promoters continued to ignore him. A Rhondda Leader journalist summed him up after his victory over Billy Padden in June:

> Triumph after triumph is being added to his remarkable record. Whether his opponent be big or small, they are treated in similar fashion. The long, raking left-handed jobs of the little collier boy, delivered with the precision and force of a piston rod, followed in a flash by a right shot with the power of miniature sledgehammer, have oft-times told its inevitable tale. Truly the greatest seven stone fighting machine the world has yet seen.

Jimmy had wanted the opportunity of fighting in London for two years and, at the end of 1913, he was still waiting. It was frustrating for him. As he enjoyed his Christmas with his family in Tylorstown, he hoped that in 1914 he would be meeting boxers in London and not depending mostly on contests in Tonypandy. Only time would tell.

CHAPTER 9

THE DREAM COMES TRUE

Jimmy was not the only person frustrated with the impasse limiting his fights to south Wales and Liverpool. Ted Lewis, who had worked hard to secure his engagements at the National Sporting Club in London and in the north of England, was absolutely dismayed. It seemed Jimmy's physical physique did not impress the bigwigs of boxing.

Ted decided to contact John Murray, the influential editor of Boxing magazine, who in turn approached 'Peggy' Bettinson at the NSC. Murray assured him that if his reason for not giving Wilde an opportunity was because of the lack of flyweight opponents, then he could quite confidently match Jimmy Wilde with men half a stone to a stone heavier. Having observed Wilde in action, John Murray ventured the opinion that there were few bantams likely to beat the Tylorstown Terror.

Bettinson was not impressed, and scoffed at his friend's remarks. His members would protest strongly if he indulged in any matchmaking which smacked of deception, he declared. As a distinguished editor and boxing expert, Murray might fancy his judgement, but it was against human nature for a lad of such low poundage to concede such a substantial weight to any opponent.

Jimmy had no choice but continue boxing in his home territory. On 3 January 1914, he was up against Kid Nutter at the Pavilion Skating Rink in Tonypandy. Born in Preston, Nutter was a riveter by trade, and was named on his birth certificate as Albert Victor

Nutter. He proved to be a difficult opponent. The Kid hardly poked his face out from behind his gloves all night. Jimmy had no option but to go to the full fifteen rounds. A month later, at the Drill Hall, Birkenhead (on 2 February), they met again with the same result.

Nutter's feat of endurance, surviving as he did for thirty rounds, has to be celebrated. Tragically, when the First World War commenced, he enlisted with the Loyal North Lancashire Fusiliers and was killed in action at High Wood on 22 July 1916. Nutter is one of the 72,337 British and South African servicemen commemorated on the Thiepval Memorial in Picardy, France. His body was never returned to Lancashire.

On 8 January, Jimmy fought fellow Welshman Young Beynon of Dowlais in Liverpool and won on points over fifteen rounds. Jimmy was back in Liverpool on 29 January, when he took on Billy Padden. The brave Padden was knocked to the floor in round three, yet four days later, he was across the Mersey in Birkenhead, where he had a sizeable number of the Birkenhead Welsh urging him on against Kid Nutter.

On 9 February, Jimmy fought Tom Thomas, who, as far as I can establish, was from Warrington It was a surprisingly common name for boxers. Between 1910 and 1940, there were at least twenty-three boxers in Britain called Tom Thomas. Most of them hailed from Wales, but this Tom Thomas was Warrington-based and his only professional fight before joining the army was against Jimmy at the Manchester Free Hall. He was badly beaten and knocked out in the seventh round.

Jimmy's next fight was against the Liverpudlian Paddy Carrol, on 12 February. Carrol's boxing career spanned from 1905 to 1915, and included thirty-three bouts in the flyweight division. Jimmy defeated him easily, knocking him out in the second round. It was Carrol's penultimate professional fight, his last being against Billy Phillips, when he lost by a knockout in front of his home fans.

On 16 February, Jimmy and Ted Lewis travelled to the Artillery

Drill Hall, Sheffield, to meet George Jaggers from Chesterfield in the bantam division. Jaggers' brief professional boxing career ran from 1910 to 1914, and the encounter with Jimmy Wilde was his career highlight. Jaggers retired three months later on 18 May 1914 at the Empress Rink, Nottingham, when he lost on points to Joe Durham. Nine of his fifteen bouts had taken place in the Skating Rink, Athletic Club, Druid Road or Bold Rodney Grounds, all of which were in his hometown. It is incredible that Chesterfield had four boxing venues and Tonypandy, a much smaller town, had three.

Ted Lewis arranged for Jimmy to return to Liverpool to meet Bill Kyne on 26 March. A professional flyweight from Poplar, London, Kyne was an excellent boxer, and during his 1907–18 career he took part in seventy-seven professional contests. In Liverpool, however, Jimmy disposed of him with a knockout in the second round to huge rejoicing from the Liverpool spectators. It had been an impressive three months, with a clean sheet. Jimmy had had eight wins between 3 January and 26 March.

Around this time, in the early part of 1914, John Murray heard of a young French fighter by the name of Eugene Husson, who was stated to scale in the region of seven and a half stone, and whose backers were excited at the prospect of matching him with the Welsh boxer. John Murray undertook to supply a fairly substantial purse, secured the Frenchman's signature to a contest, found that Wilde's backer was all for it, and was negotiating with the proprietors of the London Palladium for the hire of the hall, when Peggy Bettinson, the virtual dictator of the NSC, woke up to the situation. In spite of the extent to which John Murray's plans had developed, the match was transferred to the NSC on Bettinson's direction. It was not easy on Murray, especially as the purse offered by the Club was only about half of that first suggested for the contest. But Ted Lewis was so keen to display his boxer's wizardry at Covent Garden, while the Frenchmen were similarly dazzled by the honour extended to Husson, that they put aside their earlier commitments.

When Husson arrived in London on the Sunday before the contest, his appearance provided a huge surprise. Far from being half a stone heavier than Jimmy, as had been anticipated, he was actually about half a stone lighter. Jimmy was in his element and was confident. The task ahead was going to be easier than he had contemplated. Jimmy made full use of his golden opportunity to impress the boxing elite. He was on top form, and gave a boxing exhibition of the highest standard which convinced all those present that here was a jewel which they could not afford to neglect or lose.

Husson was to be commended for his courage, but he did not possess the boxing and fighting ability of his Welsh opponent, and certainly did not carry a punch of such destruction and power. Wilde gradually sapped his strength, and in round six the Frenchman went down on the canvas for the full count. The contest with Husson put Jimmy firmly on the road from Tylorstown to London, and, eventually, to New York. It was a golden road; his services were now in demand.

On 13 April, Jimmy met Manchester-based boxer Jack Madden at the Skating Rink Club, Ashton-under-Lyme, and won with ease. Madden was knocked out in round four. Then came the classic contest against the Frenchman Albert Bouzonnie, this time at Liverpool Stadium. Bouzonnie was a difficult opponent, rugged and tough; in the early rounds, he was well ahead on points. In fact, men of the Liverpool Welsh who were congregated around the ring sensed Jimmy was going to lose. It never happened. Bouzonnie had spent so much energy early on that, by the sixth round, Jimmy was able to land him a right to the chin which stopped him in his tracks. Bouzonnie was unable to carry on, and the contest came to an end. The large crowd roared and roared their approval of Jimmy's victory. Jimmy's name was all over the stadium.

His fourth contest in April was in the Olympia Skating Ring in Leeds against Alf Mansfield, a Londoner. Based in Aldgate, Alf had a long, distinguished boxing career of 129 bouts between 1910 and

1929. On 23 April 1913, he did well and lost to Wilde on points over twenty rounds.

Jimmy had earned his place at the National Sporting Club and he was welcomed there on the 5 May against Georges Gloria, another Frenchman. Wilde's superiority was so obvious to the NSC spectators. The Frenchman became totally exhausted and the referee was kind in stopping the contest in the ninth round. According to one newspaper account:

> Poor Gloria. The house laughed and kept on laughing, but it wasn't laughing at him. The amusement was all at Wilde. His amazing insouciance, the uncanny ease with which he did everything he felt inclined to do and the calm air of superiority with which he refrained from hurting Gloria overmuch.

As Professor Gareth Williams notes:

> Jimmy was never cruel; sometimes defeated opponents collapsed against him with their arms outstretched, and he would gently lay them out like an undertaker and walk away – this 'was one of those things which you had to laugh at'.

It was after his contest with Gloria that Jimmy read an interesting account of him by a supportive boxing writer:

> But I have lived to see the greatest – absolutely the greatest – fistic marvel of this or any other generation. Little Jimmy Wilde is the man to whom I refer, and I can safely say that he has done more than any other man in the old or modern prize or boxing ring.

He had not been able to find anyone comparable since 1719 or thereabouts. The nearest to have approached him was Ned Hunt, but Jimmy Wilde was the exception:

Never has such a thing been done or heard in the annals of the old prize ring, or in those of the modern boxing ring, and so I am fully justified in saying that Jimmy Wilde is the greatest fistic marvel the world has ever seen – and as such, I rose my hat to him.

His next contest was at the Market Hall, Aberdare, on 22 June against Charlie Banyard from Fulham, who began his career in 1913, and between then and his retirement in 1922, he fought twenty professional contests. He was no match for Wilde though, and was knocked out in the ninth round. On 18 July, Jimmy travelled to the New Marquee to meet Charlie Jordan from Jarrow in the north-east of England. Jordan had to retire in the tenth round, but at least the boxing fans of the Rhondda had seen one of the best fighters from the county of Durham. On 23 July, Jimmy returned to one of his favourite venues, namely the Liverpool Stadium, to meet Art Edwards. Edwards was popularly called an American, though he was actually a Liverpudlian; but like so many, he had lived in the United States of America for a long time. There was a close relationship at this time between Liverpool and New York. Edwards had a reputation for being an exceptionally clever boxer who had learned a great deal while he lived in the States.

Edwards was a whirlwind fighter, and he succeeded in flooring Jimmy, which was a very unusual and strange experience for the Welsh boxing genius. He also had a reputation for hitting below the belt, which is painful and also illegal. Jimmy excused him because of his small stature. He soon piled up the points and he scored in every round. The fight went to the fifteen rounds, and Jimmy was declared the winner. He pays this compliment to Liverpool and its fans:

Liverpool had taken me properly to its bosom: I had fought there as much as anywhere, and the scenes before the fight with (Edwards) were indescribable.

Thousands were packed inside the hall, while thousands clamoured for admission outside: all to see six-and-a-half stone in action! I was slowly percolating through my mind that I was becoming an 'attraction' in the real meaning of the word, and it was a grand realisation.

On 10 August, Jimmy travelled for the first time ever to St James' Boxing Hall, Newcastle upon Tyne, to meet Young Ted Walters. The two had never met in Wales, although Young Ted Walters had fought there at least twice between 17 December 1910 and 6 February 1911. Walters' first opponent had been Joe Johns, and then the superb Johnny Basham at the Public Hall, Pontnewydd, in Monmouthshire. Walters did not fight at all in 1913, and after losing to Jimmy Wilde on 10 August by disqualification, he did not fight again for nearly six years. His last professional contest was against Jimmy Morton at the City Hall, Perth, when he lost on points.

By August 1914, the boxing experts, and Ted Lewis in particular, felt Wilde was improving as a unique boxer. At Leicester's Bulwark Rink on 20 August, Jimmy met with Young Baker, an extremely clever boxer. But Wilde was on top form and provided a great evening of entertainment to boxing fans who had not seen him perform before. It was a triumph. Jimmy believed in the words of one of the old greats, Jem Mace, 'Wear your man down with your left and finish him with your right.'

In September 1914, during the early days of the First World War, David Lloyd George and the Rhondda miners' leader Mabon were among those urging miners and men of all professions to enlist in the crusade to obliterate the Kaiser and the German military might. Jimmy travelled to London to fight his second contest with Alf Mansfield on 9 September at the new West London Stadium in Marylebone. Mansfield was greatly admired by boxing reporters, a little fellow who was always full of versatility and tricks. One of the boxing correspondents maintained that:

> Mansfield was taught that he could not 'diddle' Wilde, and when he settled down to minimise the extent of his defeat, he was still outclassed (an extreme word to use when referring to Mansfield) and he would only be left to wonder how much superior Wilde was.

Mansfield was well beaten and knocked out in the tenth round. The profits for this contest were donated to the Prince of Wales Fund, and the winning gloves, as well as a dozen silk handkerchiefs, which Jimmy had signed, fetched the huge sum in those days of eighteen pounds, five shillings. The well-loved sportsman Ernest Barry bought one of these handkerchiefs and resold it to the gallery boys, which pleased Jimmy no end. For Jimmy Wilde was a real gentleman who was generous and kindhearted and who preferred to win a contest by points rather than by a devastating knockout. After the Mansfield contest, Jimmy became concerned about his right hand. He had used it so often in his booth fighting days, then in May had bruised it in his fight with Gloria. His right thumb was extremely tender, and it was discovered that the bone had been broken. This was going to prove difficult for his important contest on 16 November at the National Sporting Club against Young Joe Symonds in an eliminating fight for the Lonsdale belt. Jim Driscoll took Jimmy inside and advised him, 'Straight rights to the stomach, Jimmy, and keep him away.' That was splendid advice from a great fighter.

Young Symonds was on top form and was one of the hardest hitters at his weight, and Jimmy would be severely tested. Jimmy listened to the wise words of Driscoll, with the result that the fight went the whole of the fifteen rounds. There was no alternative – he could not risk stretching him hard with his right hand. Everyone in the Wilde camp was contented, with the prospect of Jimmy facing Sid Smith of Bermondsey in December. The winner would be in a strong position, for Sid Smith was the first boxer to be officially recognised by the boxing authorities as the British Flyweight Champion. He held the title from 1912 to 1913 and became Flyweight Champion of the World at the end of the decade. Smith was of Jewish heritage and had his first professional fight on 1 February 1907, a day before his eighteenth birthday. He defeated Joe Wilson at the NSC on 4 December 1911 to claim the first Lonsdale belt.

The fight on 3 December 1914 was scheduled for the Liverpool Stadium. Jimmy had the biggest crowd of his whole career that evening. Here in Liverpool, he was by far the favourite, but Smith had the reputation of being the ex-champion.

Jimmy had never seen Smith fight before he entered the ring with him and, in the first four rounds, they were afraid of each other. They sparred until, in round five, Smith gave the Welshman a sharp knock on the jaw, and Jimmy realised he had a difficult boxer before him. Smith moved in for the kill, and he hit Wilde as hard as he could, so Jimmy said to himself, 'He cannot knock me out!'

With that note of confidence, he responded and the contest completely changed. The crowds were excited. Smith was fighting well; he was cool and his punches were landing. In the ninth round, Smith dropped his guard for a second, and Jimmy saw his opportunity. He changed his punch to a regular hand for the jaw. Smith went down on one knee – he had been stopped in his tracks. More was to follow, and the referee had no choice but to stop the contest in the ninth round.

Elizabeth, Jimmy's wife, was at the ringside along with two comedians who had come to watch Jimmy. The first was the music-hall comedian Harry Weldon. He had come from the music hall without having changed, and he was intrigued as to who had first called her husband the Tylorstown Terror. Elizabeth told him it was Jack Scarrott. Weldon suggested, in his own words, that her husband was more of an executioner than a terror, by gum!

George Graves, another famous comedian in 1914, also came to watch the Liverpool contest. Graves had a conversation with Jim Driscoll on the merit of Wilde as the best fighter of his time. The year 1914 had been an excellent year for the Pride of the Rhondda and the future indeed looked very bright.

GREAT WELSH TRIO
JIM DRISCOLL, TOM THOMAS, FREDDIE WELSH

Duke of Windsor

Edgar Phillips

Georges Carpentier

Hugh Cecil Lowther

DIGGER STANLEY

Photo : Boxing

YOUNG SYMONDS

Tancy Lee

Photo : *Topical Press*

JOHNNY BASHAM

JIMMY WILDE

CHAPTER 10

THE FLYWEIGHT CHAMPION OF THE WORLD

In his memoir Fighting was My Business, Jimmy is full of praise for his wife's unfaltering support. Throughout his boxing career, she was the power behind the throne, preparing all his meals, helping him with day-to-day tasks and arranging his training sessions at Tylorstown. The Workmen's Institute was so proud of him, it allowed him to have a portable ring upstairs, where he was trained well by Benny Williams, the former Porth sprinter. When Jimmy wanted a break, he was able to play billiards or dominoes at the premises. It was to Tylorstown that he returned from all his travels to the north of England and London, to play golf at the Mid Rhondda Golf Club at Penrhys, and to spend time at the smallholding he shared with his father-in-law, Dai Davies, and their hundred pigeons.

For January 1915, he had been matched with James 'Tancy' Lee for the flyweight championship and the coveted Lonsdale belt. Elizabeth knew the importance of this fight, so they decided that he had to train, not at Tylorstown, but with George Baillieu at the seaside resort of Porthcawl. Elizabeth would stay at home and visit him with clean underclothes and linen once a week. Elizabeth had a huge problem with everything to do with Baillieu for she distrusted him and his whole set up in Porthcawl. She would prefer him to train as he always did back in the Rhondda. It was to be serious training as usual: the fight had been fixed for 25 January 1915, for a £500 purse. Jimmy's main sparring partner was to be Dai Matthews, the bantam pugilist from Porth. He had fought Jimmy on 8 March

1913 at Tonypandy and lost, retiring in the sixth round. The next sparring partner was Len Rowlands, and, after that, whoever volunteered.

Wilde did a great deal of road work, always accompanied by his favourite dog. Then, on the Thursday before the contest, he began to feel unwell with a stuffy, runny nose. He was certain he was coming down with the flu and looked forward to seeing his beloved Elizabeth the next day. But there was no sign of her and he began to worry she was not coming. Time dragged on, and Jimmy became convinced she was ill at home in Tylorstown. He had no way of contacting her.

Suddenly, like a breath of fresh air, she walked in, obviously angry and flushed. She had been in camp for hours, trying to get into his room. Baillieu and his wife, both of them, had lied to her, and told her Jimmy was out on a run. They knew Elizabeth would call off the fight if she knew her husband was suffering from influenza. Elizabeth left upset and with tears in her eyes, convinced that Jimmy's fight the following Monday should be called off. Baillieu and his wife were in the doghouse.

His team did their utmost to help Jimmy get better, but he still felt under the weather when he weighed in, muffled in a thick scarf and wearing an overcoat. He had a terrible headache and felt weak all over. Elizabeth had told Ted Lewis and Hughes of the situation, persuading them not to bet on her husband winning the next contest.

Lewis was adamant he should call the fight off. 'You haven't a chance!' Lewis said. 'Not a chance in a thousand, Jimmy. Be wise and call it off.' Wilde refused point-blank and suffered the consequences. He felt that the fans would be disappointed, but he had never cancelled a fight in his life. Neither did he want to upset Mr. Bettinson or Lord Lonsdale. Elizabeth arrived and told him:

Jimmy, I won't let you do it! It's crazy and foolish, and you aren't giving your backers a chance. Don't you see how it's impossible?

Wilde was adamant, although he was facing one of the best fighters from Scotland. It was to be over twenty rounds. Everything centred on Jimmy. He was responsible for the huge purse of £500 (it would otherwise have been one hundred). The Club would have been half empty without Jimmy's presence, and Bettinson was confident the fight's attendance would equal the Carpenter and Wells fight.

Jimmy did his best, and it was obvious to Ted Lewis that he would have won if he had been free of influenza. He kept on his feet and occasionally showed some of the magic and skill he was famous for. Jimmy didn't remember the fight – it was a bad dream. These are his sad, sobering words:

> I cannot tell you much about that first fight for the title. I know that after seventeen rounds I saw my seconds come through the ropes, for the referee had stopped the fight, and I was glad. I was not alert enough to be sorry. I had lost. But of the battering received, lacerating my lips badly, the right that Lee landed on my left ear caused the most damage. It was as though a steam hammer had hit me. My head rang. I went on in a daze. And the ear started to swell.

It was a wake-up call for him. He was staying that night at the Club. Elizabeth was not allowed to stay, but Ralph Lyle, the Cardiff sportsman, went to fetch her, and the rules were relaxed so she could nurse her injured husband. Jimmy's friends back in the Rhondda were so disappointed, and when he and Elizabeth arrived back in Tylorstown, his four sisters all came to welcome him at the railway station. The defeat was publicised in all the local and national press. Jimmy kept his nerve, for he knew he could regain his confidence.

They decided as a family to take a few months away from the ring. Bombadier Billy Wells advised him to spend as much time as he could on the golf course. He had played before, but now he took it seriously, and he enjoyed the daily golf (when the weather was fine) on the mid-Rhondda golf links.

Things changed. Jim Driscoll encouraged him to start training, and Benny Williams stepped in too. Baillieu was given the sack. Jimmy and Elizabeth met the comedian Charlie Austin and his wife and were invited to their houseboat at Maidenhead for a fortnight's holiday. Meanwhile, Jimmy was making a real effort to regain strength and confidence.

Tancy Lee had previously been badly beaten by Joe Symonds, a Plymouth-born boxer Jimmy had beaten in November 1914 the hard hitting Joe. Jimmy hungered for another contest with Joe Symonds, but it was not to be for the rest of 1915. Wilde spent the year travelling to meet boxers who were not in the same class as Tancy Lee or Joe Symonds, which was frustrating. Nine fights were arranged, yet the only opponent who challenged him was Johnny Best. On 25 May, Jimmy was back in Liverpool where he knew he would be welcomed with open arms for a contest with the Glaswegian Sid Shields. Shields had started his professional career on 1 July 1912, and had been knocked out two months earlier by Joe Symonds. It was the same story with Wilde, who knocked Sid Shields out in the second round of a three-minute, fifteen-round contest. The Liverpool fans were celebrating. They met again on 24 March 1917 at the Celtic Park Stadium in Glasgow in an exhibition bout before a large crowd.

On 24 July, Jimmy and his entourage visited Sheffield for a bout with Driver Benthew. It took Jimmy just five rounds to dispense with Benthew. Three weeks later, on 14 August, Jimmy met George

Clarke, a bantamweight from Bermondsey. Clarke's birth name was George Kent, but he was known in boxing circles as George Clarke. Wilde knocked him out during the eighth round.

Wilde travelled to Liverpool to meet Walter Buchanan on 23 September. Buchanan was no match for Wilde and was knocked out in the fifth round. Not long afterwards, Ted Lewis visited Jimmy in Tylorstown and asked if he would like a chance to fight in Dublin.

Jimmy answered, 'Dublin forever!' and they arranged the contest with George Cullen on 20 October. Cullen was a Dublin boxer, and he had his gloves on from 1908 until 1924. A bantamweight, he was not well known in London, or Wales for that matter. The Irish were ready for revolt against England, but Jimmy kept himself out of politics. He, Ted and the Scousers took the boat from Holyhead to Dublin, and were given a huge welcome both before the contest and after Jimmy had beaten Cullen convincingly in nine two-minute rounds. His opponent could not last the fifteen rounds and took the defeat graciously. Jimmy never went back to box in Ireland, but now he had fought in England, Scotland, Ireland and back home in the land of his fathers. He had his eyes on the distant horizon too, and was disappointed the championship remained out of his grasp.

But 1915 was not yet over, and Ted had arranged four more bouts for Jimmy. It meant travelling to Barrow-in-Furness in Cumbria. The area had a large Welsh community, particularly in Dalton- in Furness and Barrow itself. On 27 November, Jimmy was to meet Tommy Hughes of Blackburn, a boxer he'd fought in Tonypandy two years earlier, on 18 January 1913. The Palace Theatre in Barrow was packed, but Hughes proved no match for Wilde and was disqualified in the eighth round.

Jimmy's next bout was in Liverpool on 9 December against Johnny Best. The stadium was overflowing. Best was a small, stocky and thickset bantamweight who proved to be a champion fighter. He took on Tancy Lee at eight stone four pounds in April 1913. The bout showed Lee at his finest, and Best was outclassed. During 1914, Best twice met Sid Shields in ten rounds. He lost the first by a one-round knockout, and then outpointed Shield the following month. He gave Jimmy a run for his money, and lasted fourteen rounds. In the fourteenth round, Wilde gained his victory by a technical knockout. Five days later, Jimmy was expected in Bradford, another town where he had never boxed, and his opponent was Danny Elliot of Bermondsey. In his career, Elliot took part in sixty-four professional contests; however, he was no match for the Tylorstown boxer. He was literally knocked out in the second round.

Just before Christmas, Jimmy had to travel to London to meet Sid Smith. He knew Sid well. They had met nearly a year earlier in Liverpool when he was knocked out in the ninth round. This time, he was knocked out in the eighth round.

It had been a very satisfying year, except for his foolishness in fighting Tancy Lee when he was ill. Otherwise, Wilde had won every contest with flying colours and deserved to have another try at the championship. The manager of the NSC agreed. One day he asked him: 'Are you ready to fight Symonds for the championship, Jimmy?' The reply came back like a bullet: 'Whenever you like.'

Without any agreement, except a verbal exchange between Ted Lewis and Wilde, the fight was arranged for 16 February 1916 with a £500 purse given by the National Sporting Club Committee.

Elizabeth was in the kitchen in Tylorstown when Jimmy came home with the news. She was thrilled, as she felt his reputation had been unfairly dented by the Tancy Lee contest. Living at home, surrounded by his supportive family, training with Benny Williams, and attracting some of Rhondda's best sparring partners, Jimmy approached the second bid for the championship in an entirely different manner. Porthcawl had been the wrong choice as a training centre, with Baillieu a complete disaster. Elizabeth had bathed his ear daily for weeks with hot milk and it had healed (hot milk is apparently the finest cure for a swollen ear). Everyone was excited about Wilde's championship bid: the whole of the Rhondda, its MPs and dignitaries, even the Calvinistic minister of Tonypandy, Dr D. M. Phillips, who had been a power for good during the 1904–05 religious revival.

But before he met Joe Symonds, Jimmy had a few more hurdles to jump. He travelled to Swansea for 8 January 1916 to meet Billy Young Rowlands of Porthcawl, who had fought Dido Gains, George Clarke and Jack Jones. Rowlands was active between 1913 and 1920, and fought twenty-three bouts during his career. He was no match for Jimmy, and he was knocked out in the seventh round of the twenty-round contest at the Empire. Jimmy's next contest, with Tony Noble, took place on 24 January at New Cross Baths, New Cross; Noble retired in the eleventh round of a twenty-round contest, providing Jimmy with another victory. On 27 January, he faced Jimmy Morton at the stadium in Liverpool. For a fifteen round contest. Morton had no chance. He was knocked out in the second round, so it was back immediately to Tylorstown for Wilde to focus on the next fortnight of hard training before the Symonds contest. All his sparring partners were over eight stone in weight, and he was able to knock every one of them to the floor like skittles.

Jimmy travelled up to London on Sunday 13 February for the Symonds fight and, as usual, he weighed in fully dressed. The contest was attracting worldwide interest, even in the trenches of France. A large contingent from Wales would be present at the National Sporting Club.

Jimmy's hope was to bring the Lonsdale flyweight belt back to the Rhondda Fach. The trophy was valued at £300 in a twenty-round championship match. Most of the boxing critics were undecided as to what would be the result, for they felt that Joe Symonds had improved greatly since he was beaten by Sergeant Percy Jones of Porth. Wilde himself had a struggle when he fought Symonds due to an injury in his hand to win over a fifteen round highly supported boxing contest. Symonds was a boxer who loved to throw low punches, which always hurt his opponents.

He had been disqualified at the West London Stadium for issuing a low punch on Sam Keller and many in Jim's camp were concerned about his illegal punches. But after Keller's match, Symonds had beaten Digger Stanley, who was disqualified for a foul, and also George Dando, who was caught napping inside a minute.

On the other hand, Wilde had an impressive run of successes. They included wins over Johnny Best, Dan Elliott (who weighed eight stone, nine pounds), Jimmy Morton, Tom Noble, Sid Smith (first holder of the Lonsdale belt) and Billy Rowlands. All had succumbed well before the scheduled number of rounds, and although Digger Stanley told the press he strongly fancied Symonds' chances, most agreed with the *Western Mail* reporter known as C. B. that Wilde 'ought to win on points'. The only concern Jimmy had at the NSC ringside was that John Douglas was refereeing; Jim Driscoll was Wilde's chief second. Jimmy's training had gone well and he felt on top of the world. He was fighting in front of the élite of the boxing world, Lord Lonsdale, C. B. Cochran, stage stars, celebrities of London and Wales, and the dictator himself, Peggy Bettison. Nevertheless, Symonds had the advantage over him. Jimmy realised that the Plymouth-born Symonds had a better record than he had, for he had fought in more prestigious contests against boxers that Jimmy had never met. He had comfortably beaten Tancy Lee, who had badly beaten Wilde. Joe also turned the scales at eight stone against his own six stone, ten pounds in clothes, giving him a huge advantage over the man who was known as 'the Fighting Machine'.

Both knew each other's strength and weaknesses. In the first round, Symonds caught Wilde with a right to the eye that practically closed it altogether. From then on, Jimmy had only one eye with which to see Symonds, but it spurred him on. It proved to be a classic affair. Towards the end of the twelfth round, Symonds left his middle open. Jimmy delivered a right to the stomach that brought Symonds' arms down, and then he went in for the kill, delivering blows with both hands with all his skill. Joe had no choice. He went down on one knee, and then raised his hand in submission. Jimmy was glad that he didn't have to proceed with another eight rounds. The NSC was in an uproar. John Douglas lifted Wilde's arm in well-deserved victory. Johnny Basham jumped into the ring and kissed Jimmy, and Ted Lewis as well as Jim Driscoll was excited. Next day, in the visitors' room at the NSC, Bettison presented the Welsh champion with the Lonsdale belt, and paid both boxers a well-deserved tribute:

> I'd like to congratulate both the winner and the loser
> for putting up one of the finest contests ever seen at
> the Club and I think ever seen in the world.

What remained with Jimmy as he travelled back with Elizabeth to Tylorstown was the large contingent of Welshmen who had been on their feet singing the Welsh national anthem 'Hen Wlad Fy Nhadau' ('Land of my Fathers').

The rest of the year would be taken up defending his title, and concern for the war. After the contest, the Welsh-language paper *Y Darian* contained an article on the life of the mining villages, and how one would always come across a cross-section gathered in the evenings to converse and to listen to evangelists, political speakers and those who had become obsessed with boxing. The author states:

> Their heroes are Freddy Welsh and Jimmy Wilde,
> for they regard both as the two most famous Welsh
> people in the world.

Jimmy was welcomed home in style after winning the Lonsdale

belt. Hundreds of his fans and friends were waiting for him and the train at Tylorstown. Accompanying Wilde from the railway station, in a motor car kindly lent by David Morgan of Ferndale, were his father-in-law Dai Davies, David Hughes of Tonypandy, Benny Williams and Ted Lewis. The procession was led by the Ferndale Silver Prize Band, and they paraded the streets of Tylorstown, lined with cheering crowds.

They arrived at the Tylorstown Working Men's Club, where Wilde had done all his training for his contest with Symonds, and a number of speeches were delivered. Enoch Lewis presided and said how proud the Rhondda was of her boxers: Tom Thomas of Pen-y-graig, Percy Jones and Llew Edwards, both of Porth, and now Jimmy Wilde from Tylorstown. Wilde responded and paid a sincere tribute to Joe Symonds. He was 'the best boxer he had ever met', he said. Except for a black eye, he had come out of a hard battle unscathed.

Jimmy was back in London for 9 March to meet Sam Keller at the West London Stadium, Marylebone. Wilde won easily, with Keller retiring in the eighth round of a twenty-round contest. London was the place where one made money. Securing the flyweight championship had brought Jimmy Wilde prominence and some tempting offers. The theatrical manager and impresario Charles Blake Cochran secured his services, to appear after a number of rehearsals as a fully-fledged actor. Jimmy had gone to see the revue Half Past Eight. He liked it, and signed up for his appearances. Jimmy's turn in the summer of 1916 between his boxing fights was an altercation with Madame Yvonne Granville, followed by a lively boxing bout with the American Comedian Rube Welch, who weighed just over twenty stone.

Wilde's other boxing match in London was on 27 March against Sid Smith at Hoxton Baths. Smith was knocked out in the eighth round of a twenty-round contest. Returning to his home base, Jimmy was honoured at the Hippodrome, Neath, on the first Saturday in April. He was presented with a handsome marble clock subscribed by his admirers in Neath and the surrounding villages. The presentation was made by local dignitary W. B. Trick, who regarded boxing as the art of self-defence and, as a magistrate, identified with it as a 'clean, disciplined sport'. Jimmy Wilde had brought immense fame to the Welsh nation and the people of Glamorganshire were extremely proud of his skill and courage. Trick, in presenting the clock, said:

> Long may you live to hear it tick, but when you are down, I hope you will be able to get up within the tick of ten seconds.

Jimmy was caught off the hop by Trick's words. He blushed vividly and confessed he much preferred to box than to make a speech. His response went down well.

On 24 April at Liverpool Stadium, he defended his IBU flyweight title against Johnny Rosner, another powerful flyweight. Rosner was no match for Jimmy, and retired in the eleventh round of a twenty-round contest. Five days later, on 29 April, Jimmy was fighting Benny Thomas at the Empire Theatre, Cardiff. Thomas had fought Sam Mainwaring of Pontardawe here and won, but this time his luck was out. Thomas stayed the fifteen rounds, but lost on points. Later that year, on 26 August, the Swansea Valley weekly paper *Llais Llafur* in August 1916. reported on Benny Thomas's death: he was killed in action.

Jimmy was back at the Empire on 13 May to meet Joe Magnus in a six-round contest. Magnus was unable to match him as Benny Thomas had done a fortnight earlier and was knocked out in the second round. Darkey Saunders proved no match for him either, for he too was knocked out in the third round of a six-round contest. This led Wilde to his most important boxing event of the year on 26 June 1916 at the National Sporting Club. He was again facing

Tancy Lee, who had beaten him on 25 January 1915 for the vacant British, European and IBU World flyweight titles. Their second encounter proved very different. Wilde kept clear of Lee's powerful punches and, this time, it was Lee who was in trouble. Jimmy stopped him early in the eleventh round of a twenty-round contest with a right to the chin, which resulted in him retaining the IBU and British flyweight titles and gaining the European Boxing Union title. The NSC had put up a stake of £500, with side stakes of £250. Lord Lonsdale was in the chair to see the victorious Wilde being congratulated.

Jimmy stayed in London after the victory, for it had been arranged that he was to visit the Houses of Parliament at Westminster on 29 June. Ted Lewis accompanied him, and over one hundred Members of Parliament met Jimmy to congratulate him on the victory. The Duke of Buccleuch greeted them with a speech in the Gilded Chamber of the House of Lords before they were led to the House of Commons. The Welsh MPs were excited to join him, and John Hinds, the Liberal MP for West Carmarthenshire, led him around the House. Will Crooks, the veteran Labour MP, met him in the inner lobby. Crooks had been an amateur boxer and was very keen on the sport. The biggest shock of the visit was when Jimmy met the Liberal MP for Merthyr Tydfil, Edgar Jones. Jones had forgotten, until Jimmy reminded him, that he had taught Jimmy in the school at Tylorstown before he entered the House of Commons.

Edgar Jones soon remembered the small, cheeky boy who was always ready with his hands. He admitted to fellow politician Geoffrey Howard that he had taught Jimmy to 'take a lot of punishment'. Jimmy also met W. Llewellyn Williams, the MP for Carmarthen Boroughs. Williams was a distinguished legal expert, and he and Jimmy had met in the company of Dr Arthur Alfred Lynch a Member for West Clare in Ireland, representing the Irish Parliamentary Party in the House of Commons. Lynch was an intriguing Irish Australian civil engineer who was also a medical doctor, well versed in boxing, had made all the arrangements for the visit of the famous boxer, and who raised a private battalion of the Munster Fusiliers in 1916 to fight on the side of Britain. This was wartime, and a number of wounded soldiers had been invited to shake hands with Jimmy, displaying an obvious delight in meeting him. Though tired, Jimmy realised the visit's importance rested on the interest Britain's leaders were taking in boxing.

Jimmy's next contest was against Johnny Hughes at Kensal Rise Athletic Club, Kensal Green, where he fought for and retained all his titles. Hughes was knocked out in the tenth-round of a twentyround contest.

Afterwards, it was a joy for Jimmy to be able to spend the summer months at home in Tonypandy, as he had so many commitments and so many animals to care for. His best friends in the animal world were Bess, a Labrador retriever, and Jim, a devoted Airedale terrier. Jimmy's second son was born in 1916 and was named Verdun after the famous battle of that year.

On 9 November, Jimmy faced the fierce Tommy Noble in Liverpool. He was knocked off his feet by the other man, but recovered. The fight lasted fifteen rounds of a twenty-round contest. Jimmy was not at his best that night, but only he, Ted Lewis and his trainers knew the reason.

Elizabeth Wilde always prepared his food as he was a huge eater. One evening, before travelling to Liverpool, she took issue with some prepared brawn. Jimmy was annoyed and lost his temper. He had a terrible temper at times, as unruly travellers on the train between Cardiff and Paddington often found out. On this occasion, Elizabeth prepared fresh salmon for him instead.

A few hours later, everyone who had eaten the brawn was reeling in pain. Their six-year-old son David collapsed, as did the family's live-in maid. They were suffering from food poisoning, caused by the brawn and their symptoms lasted fifty hours. If Jimmy had gone ahead and eaten the brawn, he would not have been able to travel to Liverpool or fight with Noble. Food poisoning would also have weakened him for his most important fight of 1916: facing Young Zulu Kid, a prominent Italian-American boxer, at Holborn Stadium in London.

The boxer's real name was Giuseppe Di Melfi. He was born in Italy but had gone to the United States with his family as a child. Kid was nicknamed 'Fighting Newsboy' and he had only lost one fight. The contest against Jimmy Wilde was promoted by Jack Callaghan, with the two men competing for the world flyweight title. Jimmy went home to train, for he had lost a great deal of his livestock in a snowstorm that had brought the Rhondda valleys to a standstill. In Tonypandy, he had five first-class sparring partners in Billy Fry, Jack Josephs, Gomer Evans, Dai Davies and George Jones. They were all nine stone, and excellent boxers and strong men; however, they admitted they would be glad when Jimmy and the Kid were in the ring. Ted Lewis was always at hand, doing it all from the goodness of his heart.

But it took a while for them to persuade Ted Lewis, who had so many other interests, to accept his fair percentage from the purse for all he was doing for the Rhondda boxers, namely Llew Edwards, Percy Jones and Jimmy Wilde.

Jimmy was confident when he left for London. Elizabeth said he was 'chirpy' like a bird. In the weigh-in, he got on well with his fellow flyweight Zulu Kid. The contest was an exciting one for the large crowd, who had come to watch the two best flyweights in the whole world. Jimmy did not spare the visitor – he threw punch after punch, until Zulu Kid was clutching the rope, or slowly getting onto his feet from the floor, clearly hurt and confused.

A right to the chin hurt him until he groaned, and his legs bended.

Zulu Kid was in trouble, swaying helplessly, with his hands too tired to throw a punch far. To be fair to him, he had managed to land some very heavy punches to Jimmy's stomach and chest, which had repercussions. In the eleventh round, however, Zulu Kid was in trouble and the referee intervened. Jimmy had won the championship.

Jimmy Wilde's dream had been fulfilled. The world championship was in his hands, and would remain so for years to come. He was happy, but first he needed medical care. as a consequence of the fight against Tancy Lee. In April 15 he began his suffering a great deal and his ill health had cost him dearly financially. He had been a shadow of himself when he faced Tancy Lee and had never properly recovered. His earlier defeat had lost him engagements in music halls amounting to over £2,000 and he was also offered £1,000 if he allowed the promoter of the Liverpool Stadium to book a contest rather than allowing Lile to have the opportunity. He had also cancelled a match with Dido Gains of London.

Jimmy went into a private nursing home, where the foremost medical man of his generation, Sir Herbert Barker, restored him to full health, though the army authorities were struggling with his application to join the colours.

Jimmy had appeared before the recruiting medical board in Cardiff in May 1916, when his plea to be a soldier was refused on the grounds that 'he is underweight standard, and not likely to make an efficient soldier'. He had been previously rejected in Birmingham, as a 24-year-old, for after all he was only five feet two inches in height. Jimmy appealed. After beating Zulu Kid, and with a clean bill of health, he appeared again in front of the medical board at Cardiff. It was the same old problem: he simply did not weigh enough as a boxer or a soldier.

In January 1917, Jimmy appeared before the Rhondda Recruiting

Tribunal at Porth and applied for leave to appeal as he had not done so within the prescribed period. He informed them he had worked as a miner for ten years, and that he had been rejected medically on two previous occasions. In his opinion, he would be more useful in a war crisis situation if he went back to his old colliery: his father, two sisters, two brothers, his wife and two children were very much dependent financially on him. As a boxer, he was the family breadwinner. The Chairman W. P. Nicholas asked him: 'You would have then a good time in the army?' Jimmy Wilde replied, 'Yes, if they would keep my family.'

Nicholas said Jimmy's application would be dealt with in due course, but that he didn't expect him to be given his freedom as a boxer. The country needed men to serve within the army. Cardiff had a different approach; Jimmy was given the all-clear and placed in Class B1, meaning the garrison or provisional duty abroad. This placed him in a difficult position. Much pressure and propaganda were being exerted on men to join up. In 1916, the Prime Minister David Lloyd George had got the Military Service Act through parliament. The legislation gave those who were healthy no option but to join up. Wilde presented himself for more than one re-examination because he was tired of taunts from those who thought he should be in army uniform, despite him being rejected more than once.

Jimmy was looking forward to being in Edinburgh from 1 to 13 January 1917. On 29 January he planned to meet George Clarke at the National Sporting Club to defend his flyweight title. The following day, he would be wearing the uniform proud that he was to be counted among his working-class friends, all the miners he knew, who had no choice but face active service. He was heading to Aldershot, where he would work as a physical instructor alongside his great friends and fellow Welsh boxers Jim Driscoll and Johnny Basham, now both army sergeants.

CHAPTER 11

ARMY DAYS

In Aldershot, Jimmy felt homesick, and felt a huge amount of hiraeth for Elizabeth and his close-knit family. He wrote to her often, one day asking her to come and meet him at Reading. She could come on the Great Western line from Cardiff and he would meet her at the railway station. He managed to procure a motorbike, though he had no experience of riding. On a practice run the day before her arrival, Jimmy arrived at the station and could not stop the bike. He went round and round the entrance of the station, finally making a dive for it before the bike seized up. He had learnt a lesson. The next day, he went on foot to meet his darling Elizabeth.

It was around this time that Jack Johnson, the black American heavyweight, asked Jimmy to take his part in a revue called 'Seconds Out', as he had to go back to the United States. The two men were very fond of each other, but Jimmy was unable to oblige. He was in the middle of his training to be a physical instructor.

Unsurprisingly, he passed easily, and was handed a certificate to prove he had completed his training. The time had gone quickly and, while he was training, he had been surrounded by boxers of the calibre of Bombardier Billy Wells, Johnny Basham, Pat O'Keefe, Ernie Barry and Jim Driscoll. On one particularly exciting day, Bombardier Billy Wells and Jimmy Wilde staged a boxing exhibition at the camp. Billy was a tall man, and Jimmy was just over five foot. Billy swiped while Jimmy tucked and weaved and kept out of harm's way.

Jimmy was sent from Aldershot to Sandhurst. The army authorities did everything to ensure his comfort – they were proud to have him as a physical instructor. Elizabeth was able to come from Tylorstown and rent a small house near Sandhurst College, and she brought the sons David and Verdun with her. Jimmy was invited to box in front of David Lloyd George and his wife Margaret at the Alhambra Theatre during a Welsh-themed matinée on 24 February 1917.

An important fight at the National Sporting Club was on the horizon. Jimmy was facing George Clarke on 12 March and there was an excellent purse for a twenty-round contest. Clarke had beaten all champions and challenges, and was willing to fight Wilde at between eight stone two pounds and eight stone four pounds, with a reputation even with all the advantage, George Clarke was no match for the Mighty Atom and was knocked out in the fourth round of a twenty-round contest.

Jimmy was on top of the world. He had tried eight times to get into the British Army. Seven times he had been rejected because he was under the height, and weighed only 98 pounds. He tried to stretch out an inch or two and ate huge meals, but still he remained a mere 100 pounds. The army recognised he could be a boxing instructor of the first order and allowed him to take part in occasional boxing contests. They knew he was the disciple of Jim Driscoll, the master of the 'one-two' punch, which was now the speciality of Jimmy Wilde and had seen George Clarke fall to the ground in round four.

It was an astonishing punch, as George Clarke had found out. Captain Tom Flanagan, who was in charge of the Canadian boxers stationed in Aldershot and Sandhurst, arranged bouts so that they could see Jimmy in action. The captain would tell his inexperienced boxers to take it easy with the Welsh Mighty Atom until the final round. He argued that if you upset him with a punch, he would fight with double power and speed. Prior to joining the British Army and heading to Aldershot, Jimmy had fought eightynine ring battles. He had won forty-seven with knockouts (most of them in the third round), had won twenty-nine as a result of a decision, and had drawn three bouts. In 1915, he won eight and lost one to Tancy Lee in seventeen rounds, but Lee was a bantamweight boxer. In 1916 and 1917, Jimmy Wilde knocked out three in eleven rounds, and won sixteen fights – most of them with knockouts. In 1918, he won three fights and lost one on a four-round decision to Memphis Pal Moore.

Then, on 22 March, at the Holborn Stadium, Wilde met Jimmy Russell. It is interesting to note that Russell was a professional boxer for only two years, from 1918 to 1919, and took part in just seven contests. The fight with Wilde was one of the seven, and he lost, being knocked out in the third round of a fifteen-round contest.

For the remainder of 1917 – indeed until March 1918 – Jimmy was busy meeting interesting individuals in the army camps. His superior officer was Captain John Hopley, who was six foot four and weighed nearly sixteen stone. Hopley was a gentle giant who was educated at the University of Cambridge.

One celebrity at Sandhurst was Prince Henry, the third son of King George and Queen Mary. Though Henry excelled at sport, he was not keen on being involved in boxing, preferring tennis. But the Prince did watch the exhibition match between Jimmy and Corporal Jacobs, one of the few that he saw.

On 28 March, Jimmy met Corporal Jacobs, a native of Hampshire. It was Jacobs' only boxing bout and Jimmy scared the life out of him. Jacobs only lasted four rounds of the six-round contest at the Headquarters Gymnasium in Aldershot. Four weeks later, on 29 April, Jimmy boxed against Dick Heasman at the NSC in defence of his British and lineal flyweight titles.

Heasman was from Lambeth, and had only started his professional career the previous year on 7 May. His career as a flyweight was short (1917–20); however, during that time he fought some excellent

Welsh fighters. For example, he fought Lewis Williams from Pen-y-Graig as well as Tommy Davies, and he had three bouts with Tal Jones of Maesteg. In April 1918, he faced the greatest of them all, Jimmy Wilde. His team threw in the towel in the second round of a twenty-round contest. Jimmy retained both titles easily.

Later that month, Jimmy boxed at an exhibition at Covent Garden with one of the great boxers, the ex-bantamweight champion Thomas 'Pedlar' Palmer. Despite being nearly forty, Pedlar fought well. The NSC's directors had invited a number of American soldiers and sailors to the exhibition and hosted a lavish dinner. The speakers included the distinguished barrister and politician Sir F. E. Smith (later Lord Birkenhead), Admiral Sims and General Biddle, Lord Burnham (owner of the Daily Telegraph) and Sir Walter de Frece. Peggy Bettinson spoke at the ringside in praise of the boxers.

Jimmy realised the army authorities did not approve of staging a boxing match for money. London promoter Jerry Cripps, Dan Sullivan and Dick Burge had arranged for Jimmy to meet Joe Conn, the nine-stone boxer, who was reckoned by many a boxing expert to be the best man at his weight in the British Isles.

The contest was to be staged at the Chelsea Football Ground at Stamford Bridge on Saturday, 31 August 1918.

Joe Conn (his birth name was Joseph Cohen) had boxed against Billy Fry of Tylorstown on 2 October 1915. Fry went on to become the Welsh Area Welterweight Champion for 1930–31, but on 29 April 1918 he was fighting Conn again, winning on points over twenty rounds in Blackfriars. The result offered some comfort to Jimmy, but not a lot; Conn had the advantage of nearly two stones and Jimmy knew his own reach did not equal the Londoner's.

Jimmy trained hard, helped by two Welsh boxers. One was Young Charles of Newport, a welterweight and a humorous lad. Jimmy confessed in his autobiography:

I often grew disgruntled during the period of training. I would have been lost without Charles and his fooling many a time.

His other sparring partner was a Welsh-speaking boxer from Ammanford called Idris Jones. Jones, like Conn, was a nine stone pugilist. Captain Hopley was also an inspiration, and together the three men kept Jimmy in shape.

As Jimmy Wilde expected, the military refused to authorise the contest, as did the British Boxing Board of Control (it did not fall under their auspices). There is no doubt it would have been cancelled had the Right Honourable George Barnes, a Labour Party politician, not used his influence with Lloyd George and the coalition cabinet. Thanks to Barnes, the contest was allowed to take place, but Jimmy was afraid the army would not allow him to leave Sandhurst.

Jimmy sent off a decoy party with Elizabeth and Idris Jones, and he stepped on to the train at Farnborough. He was not rebelling, for he had been allowed leave of absence, but he was afraid the whole costly affair would amount to nothing. He knew Sullivan and Burge had placed £2,000 (a huge sum in 1918) on Joe Conn. Discussing the fight with Elizabeth beforehand, Jimmy concluded his tactic should be to make Conn miss him as often as he could.

The critics would be annoyed, but Conn's weight meant he would have very little advantage.

The day of the fight was to be remembered for another reason: the first and biggest police strike in cities like London and Liverpool (there was a second, much smaller strike the following year). Jerry Cripps took control, and arranged for seven hundred men in light hospital blue to make a circle around the ring. They were replacing the police!

In the first four rounds, Conn was kept away from the smaller man.

Jimmy did attack now and again, but he kept out of reach until the fifth round. Conn landed several heavy blows on his face, and cut his lip severely. He was energised, and he reopened a cut on Wilde's left eye. It was a distressing scene, and Conn was gaining ground in every round. Though Conn was missing a large number of powerful punches, and Jimmy was missing more, Jimmy realised during the tenth round that 'Big Joe' was tiring fast and he reverted to his usual tactics. Wilde went for the giant, and Conn went down to the floor six times in round ten, before the bell came to his rescue.

Making a game show in the next round, Joe spent a lot of time going down and getting up; however, it was the twelfth round which saw the finish. With Conn on the floor for the third time, the referee had no choice but to intervene. The Stepney lad had been punished enough, and the bout was stopped, with the verdict naturally going to Tylorstown's Mighty Atom.

The open-air contest did not draw the anticipated crowds, although the cheapest seats were well patronised. The upper classes stayed away, though had such a bout been staged at the Olympia, it would likely have drawn a record gate that would have stood for decades. But more crucial in the long term was the decision by the army authorities, before the fight, that boxers in the services would be banned from receiving purse money. To overcome this difficulty, the promoters awarded Wilde and Conn a bag of diamonds each, which they promptly turned into cash at the first opportunity. After the fight, Jimmy announced that, in view of the decisions and feelings of the military towards its servicemen and boxing, he would not fight again while he was in the army. In fact, he did not put on his gloves in serious combat until a month after the armistice, when the well-publicised International Tournament for the King's Trophy was staged at the Royal Albert Hall. Boxers from every branch of the services and each of the allied countries took part in this memorable festival, and Jimmy Wilde was called to represent the British Army in the bantamweight class. He outpointed the American Joe Lynch, who went on to become the World Bantamweight Champion, in the second round of the tournament., and the Australian Digger Evans in the semi-finals. His opponent in the final was Pal Moore and, though the troops of the different nations considered Wilde had won by a comfortable points margin, the judges and referee gave their verdict in favour of Moore.

The decision in the American's favour temporarily stunned the audience of ten thousand, but when it was realised that Wilde had been adjudged the loser, there was a tremendous uproar. The rest of the show was held up by the volume of boos and catcalls coming from around the arena and directed at the judges and referee.

The din was so great that, when the next two boxers entered the ring, the Master of Ceremonies was unable to make himself heard. In desperation, Jim Driscoll was sent for, and it was not until Peerless Jim climbed through the ropes and held up his hands that the vast audience was persuaded to quieten down.

'Ladies and gentlemen,' said Driscoll, swallowing hard the whole time. 'As trainer of the British Army team, I am quite satisfied [here he took a big gulp] with the decision, and I may say so is Wilde.' Jimmy was far from being satisfied; however, he never questioned his mentor, trainer and friend's successful peacemaking efforts. With his conciliatory words, Driscoll had deftly prevented the situation from escalating into a violent, ugly scene.

In March 1919, Jimmy Wilde resumed his professional career as a boxer, and for the first time he was bringing in really big money. The First World War had brought several big-scale promoters into the sport, and the National Sporting Club was beginning to feel the pinch after its lengthy reign. Moreover, the NSC had been slow in recognising the talents of Jimmy Wilde.

Wilde's last contest at the NSC was on 31 March, when he faced Joe Lynch again. This proved to be another extremely important historic occasion. Lynch possessed a hard right hand. He would often fight as Jimmy had done, twice a week. Bouts with Memphis Pal Moore, Abe Goldstein, Jack Sharkey and Pete Herman propelled him to the top of his division. Lynch had been in the navy when he'd boxed with Wilde at the Royal Albert Hall. Now, in the National Sporting Club, he proved to be a difficult boxer to beat, and Jimmy only won by a very narrow margin.

In Lynch, Jimmy was meeting a first-class performer and one who, having had slight experience of the famous Welshman's unorthodox style, had taken the lesson to heart. On 31 March, Lynch employed tactics designed to cope with any moves Jimmy might make. Likely, Wilde's continuous attacking gave him the verdict, but the points margin in his favour must have been extremely narrow. Joe Lynch gave a brilliant, outstanding exhibition of strategic fighting, and finished by far the fresher of the two boxers. Afterwards, the Prince of Wales (later to become King Edward VII and then the Duke of Windsor and a huge friend of Jimmy's) stepped into the ring, shook the hands of both men, and congratulated them on a thrilling and sportsman-like performance.

For a member of the royal family to make such a close contact with the glove game was a grand moment for boxing, and the Welsh nation. Indeed, there is a famous oil painting by William Howard Robinson titled *A Welsh Victory at the National Sporting Club, 31st March 1919*, which keeps afresh and alive the memory of that famous boxing match.

Jimmy's next match was in his favourite city Liverpool on 21 April 1919. His opponent was Jimmy Buck, who hailed from Stockport originally but was living in Castlefield. Buck had never fought in Wales. Buck was no Joe Lynch and Jimmy was not stretched by the Yorkshire-based boxer. Buck was knocked out in the third round of a fifteen-round contest and Wilde returned to Tylorstown with an easy victory.

A few days later, he returned to the Stadium Club in Holborn, London, to do battle with a far better boxer than Jimmy Buck: Alf Mansfield. Mansfield had already gone the distance with Wilde some six years previously, and there was nothing in his subsequent record to suggest he would give the Welshman the fight he did. Jimmy found him an easy target, and started to punish him as early as the first round. He even dropped Mansfield in the second round for a count of eight and damaged his features considerably. After five rounds, Mansfield had taken sufficient punishment to make most boxers throw in the towel. He, however, was a man of sterner stuff. When he should have left the ring in the opinion of the critics, Mansfield surprised everyone, and most of all Jimmy Wilde and Ted Lewis, by staging a great attack and forcing the Welshman to fight at close range. Now Jimmy, in a long, distinguished career, was never one for in-fighting; however, this time, he had no option. Mansfield pressed him hard, and drove him into the ropes for long spells of close-quarter work. Jimmy, the greatest boxer in the world, was, for a while, very much at sea and in dire trouble.

After the ordeal of being roughly handled for several rounds, Wilde decided the only option was to outpunch Mansfield. The spectators were on the edge of their seats as they witnessed these exciting exchanges from two driven boxers. Eventually, the hard-hitting Wilde came out on top. He had conquered the Londoner at last, and, in the eleventh and twelfth rounds, Mansfield was humiliated and delivered to the floor. In the thirteenth round, Jimmy went for a verdict, for he had no intention of fighting fifteen rounds with Alf Mansfield. The referee and Mansfield's seconds acted simultaneously to bring the contest to a close. Wilde had once more demonstrated to his British fans that he was indeed the Tylorstown Terror.

Jimmy had the whole of May and June and most of July to be well prepared for his next huge fight at the Olympia in Kensington, London. The date was fixed for 17 July, and his opponent was none other than Memphis Pal Moore, the boxer who had gained the lucky decision over Jimmy in the King's Trophy tournament. Wilde and Moore were matched to box twenty rounds, and this time there was no doubt who was the superior boxer. Jimmy had trained hard on Penrhys mountain and in his gym at Tylorstown. Moore was an extremely clever boxer; he was fast on his feet and he possessed a variety of heavy punches and clever moves. Moore was almost as adept at covering up as Jimmy, but his distinctive boxing skill was the way he slapped with the open glove, despite this breaking the rules of the game. Time after time, Moore appeared to catch Wilde with a heavy swing, and although these blows certainly knocked Jimmy off his balance from the sheer weight behind them, they made more noise than they caused damage.

Wilde was never, for even a moment, in any danger from the American. The Welshman boxed in his well-known style, dancing on, shooting straight punches with either hand, covering, ducking – in fact, buzzing round Moore like a wasp. He seemed to place his punches from almost any angle, and waited patiently as his opponent covered himself up with his hands. Wilde was clever. He would find a slight hole in Moore's defence through which he could shoot one of his stinging deliveries.

Wilde's victory over Memphis Pal Moore, although won on points over twenty tiring rounds, was exactly what he needed to further his career. He had at last been made an attractive offer to tour America and Canada during the coming winter. His victory over Moore, coming immediately after his win over Lynch, was sufficient to provide him with all the advance publicity he could possibly require. No British boxer in 1919 had more value to the Americans than Jimmy Wilde. The sport had never seen a greater fighter at the flyweight or even bantamweight division. The Welshman was the first unified world flyweight champion, not only beating the best boxers of Britain and Europe, but also the Americans he had met in London.

Such was Wilde's skill that he was confident enough to take on bigger men; after all, he had defeated Joe Lynch and Memphis Pal Moore on points. Wilde had even stepped up to the featherweight division to completely destroy the British champion Joe Conn. He was a marvel, and the Americans were looking forward to the visit of the Mighty Atom. Jimmy could hammer his opponents. This was the man who had defeated nearly one hundred boxers. Being hard to hit, he had become a legend in his lifetime. How could anyone defeat this tiny titan who was willing to fight twenty rounds with heavier men?

Pete Herman was gracious enough to claim that:

> "Wilde is the greatest boxer that I have ever seen. I was in better condition for the fight than I have ever been in before".

Jimmy had a tremendous time after the victory over Pal Moore. He delighted his admirers at the Rhondda Golf Clubhouse on 18 July with a smart display at the billiard table, in which he made a record break of fifty-five. The previous record for the clubhouse was forty-nine.

He had a number of exhibition bouts in October in cities like Norwich and back home in Wales. On 16 October, crowds flocked to the mining village of Caerau, near Maesteg, where Jimmy had promised to fight in the Coliseum. C. B. Thomas, a huge admirer of the so-called Tylorstown Terror, had erected a proper ring on the stage, which he did for all Jimmy's exhibition bouts attended that summer and autumn. Unfortunately, Jimmy was late arriving; his car had broken down while he was motoring the long distance back from Norwich. At eight o'clock, the master of ceremonies announced that the party had left Newport and would be at Caerau by nine o'clock. 'Little Jimmy' received an enthusiastic ovation and boxed two rounds each with two promising lads from the locality:

Cynwyd Jenkins and Tal Jones. Everyone in the Coliseum enjoyed the boxing skill and the cleverness of Jimmy Wilde.

Jimmy had signed for the American tour soon after being demobilised in 1919 and his experience fighting the American boxer Pal Moore had made him anxious to fulfil the contract. The purse for their match had been huge, at £5,000, which worked out as £3,000 for the winner and £2,000 for the loser, plus a side stake of £1,000. Before and during the war, the biggest purse had been £2,000.

During 1919, Wilde went over to Paris to box in a fête promoted by the French refugees, and during the event fought an exhibition with Georges Carpentier. The crowd was in a good mood – ten thousand of them – and Jimmy was cheered for at least five minutes. In England, Wales and Paris, he had heard more applause for an exhibition bout than for a real fight, which, in his opinion, indicated that the spectators preferred boxing to fighting. After the exhibition, he went out with George and his wife, Tom Webster, and two other friends.

Then, at last, Jimmy was ready to travel to the 'paradise of boxing', namely the United States of America. No British boxer had ever been accepted in world boxing circles until he had been to the States. Jimmy's team included his wife Elizabeth. David Hughes travelled as Wilde's manager (instead of Ted Lewis) along with his trainer Benny Williams. Benny had been with him for years and could be relied upon for expert advice and general assistance. The Prince of Wales could not allow him to travel without meeting him and they spent fifteen minutes together on 28 November. Then Jimmy Wilde and his team boarded the White Star liner Baltic in Liverpool to face their three-thousand-mile journey.

Jimmy Wilde

Nat Fleischer

Quakers Yard

Jack Dempsey

Joe Calzaghe

Jim Driscoll (Peerless Jim)

Theodore Roosevelt

William Abraham

Rhondda Fach

Wilkie Bard

CHAPTER 12

THE NEW WORLD BOXING EXPERIENCE

The voyage to North America proved a difficult one. Conditions at sea were dreadful, and, after the first day, Jimmy spent most of his time in the sick berth. David Hughes and Benny were equally seasick; however, Elizabeth – who had never been on a lengthy ocean voyage before – was fine.

They reached Halifax, where Elizabeth went shopping and returned with a new lady friend. She told her husband: 'Jimmy, this is Mrs. Roberts from – you would never guess – Tylorstown!'

Mrs. Roberts had recognised Elizabeth Wilde and introduced herself. She then took the couple home to her flat for tea and to meet her Canadian husband. They had married during the war. Both Jimmy and his wife had known her as a little girl in the Rhondda. They were all delighted.

After Halifax, they headed to New York, where Elizabeth had no intention of staying in a hotel. After a great deal of anxiety, they finally found a place for the Welsh contingent to stay. She had brought her own supply of goodies and insisted on doing the cooking, for a change of diet could have caused problems for her champion. Their new abode was a home from home.

Heavyweight Jack Bloomfield became a frequent visitor, while T. O. Williams, a businessman from Cardiff, travelled all the way from Canada to see Jimmy in action.

Jimmy immediately encountered the bureaucracy of the International

Sporting Club. He was to face Jack Sharkey of New York at the Cream City Athletic Club's Auditorium, under the management of Otto Borchert, the club's president, in Milwaukee, Wisconsin, on 6 December. He and his team were preparing to travel from New Jersey to Milwaukee when the Prince of Wales – who had arrived in New York Harbour on HMS Renown – asked them to visit him. The prince was glad to see them and happily signed Elizabeth's autograph book. He wished Jimmy well. 'I wish I could stay for the Sharkey match, but I must get back. I'll leave you to show America what you can do!'

The unexpected royal visit meant they missed the train, and it was bitterly cold when they finally arrived in Milwaukee. They found a place to stay at Wauwatosa, five miles from downtown Milwaukee. The Milwaukee Athletic Club hosted a luncheon in Jimmy Wilde's honour and invited him to train at their gymnasium, another honour. He was a Welshman and so was made to feel at home. There was a wave of anti-English sentiment in a city where there was a large Irish immigrant community. Jimmy was very surprised at the lack of tolerance shown when Jack Bloomfield had a Union Jack around his waist, the Irish exiles became hysterical and he had no choice but take it off. He could not believe his ears at the prejudice against the English that came from the lips of those that he met and he was glad that the Welsh Americans were less aggressive towards the English folk.

Jimmy was fortunate in having a strong Welsh accent and he displayed the Welsh dragon in his training rather than a Union Jack! On the morning of the fight, snow prevented him going for a round of golf, something Jimmy liked to do before an evening contest. He drank some egg-and-milk with Al Thompson, his chief sparring partner. Elizabeth believed that the drink was drugged, for Jimmy reeled back to the house in Wauwatosa feeling giddy and violently sick. Al was also ill. In fact, he did not recover for a long time, and when he did he badly lost his contest.

Jimmy realised that the boxing rules varied from state to state. But another factor that differed greatly was the method of counting points, and the habit of American referees of making a bout a 'no decision' one, leaving it to sports reporters to explain the contest to their readers.

To the great dismay of Jimmy's British followers, the newspapers decided that, in spite of the fact Wilde had fought like a tiger from beginning to end, he was unable to cope with Sharkey's superior reach and his huge advantage of eight and a half pounds in weight. They gave Jimmy only the first round, made the fifth, sixth and eighth even, and decided that Sharkey had won the rest.

Sharkey had upset everyone in Jimmy's camp, and Elizabeth was furious that her husband had been poisoned. Even so, Wilde earned $11,000 for the Sharkey battle, so he was well pleased. It was not a glorious start to a huge adventure, but he was not dismayed. He was in America to make money and had started well enough – only six years earlier he had been earning a pittance as a miner.

After the fight, Sharkey admitted to the American boxer James J. Corbett:

> He's the shiftiest, cleverest little fellow I ever saw. He will trim any fellow that tries to box it with him because he is a master there. I beat him because I wouldn't fight his way – I wouldn't box him. Slugging – that's my game. It isn't his. As a result, he was forced into battling methods with which he was not at all familiar.

It was a fair and balanced comment from the victorious boxer. Jimmy and his team could look forward to Christmas in the States before travelling to St Louis in the new year to fight Babe Asher. The date was set for 8 January and Wilde trained in Milwaukee.

Johnny 'Babe' Asher, a bantamweight champion, was only twenty years of age when he stepped into the ring at the Coliseum to face Jimmy Wilde, flyweight champion of the world, and a veteran boxer of twenty-eight years of age with a record of 298 knockouts. Wilde had attracted more attention than any boxer of his day except world heavyweight champion Jack Dempsey; however, the contest with Jack Sharkey had tarnished Wilde's reputation with his American fans. Nevertheless, Jimmy was regarded as the perfect boxing stylist, and according to the sporting editor of the St Louis Post Dispatch, John E. Wray, 'he combines with his skill perfect poise, coolness, wonderful generalship and a knock-out punch in his right hand'.

Asher had fought forty-two contests, so he didn't possess the boxing experience of the Welshman. The referee was Walter Heisner and Wilde would receive $5,000. Asher would also get a percentage. But Asher had to weigh 116 pounds for the eight rounds before seven thousand fans. Since leaving the USA Army, Asher had fought six contests against some very well round boxers... Twice he had beaten Zulu Kid and Wilde had won in a title bout over Kid.

Now Babe Asher was meeting the master. This time, Wilde completely rehabilitated himself in American eyes, and after flooring Asher on three occasions, it was generally agreed by the American press that he had won hands down. They had seen the world's greatest boxer in action.

John E. Wray wrote:

> This young Welshman is one of the greatest heroes the square circle has ever known. The ring is his field of battle; his sword is a five-ounce glove; the count is the grim death rattle of the foes he stands above. He is an ideal champion, and it is no wonder that the English are wild about Wilde, for this fellow stands like an eagle on a lofty peak above the crowds, buzzards, jackdaws and sparrows of the ring.

Asher must be given credit for his courage, for 'he boxed as if he might have had St Vitus's dance!' Wray adds:

> Wilde nailed him and Asher went down. He was also
> badly stunned in the fifth and flattened in the sixth.
> He staggered though the seventh and eighth, but was
> a badly beaten boy– beaten but not dishonoured.

Referee Heisner had no hesitation in adding to the glorious appreciation of the Welshman: 'Wilde is the greatest two-fisted boxer I have ever seen. Pay him that tribute because it is deserved.'

Heisner was not referring only to boxers in the flyweight division. For him, Wilde was 'the greatest two-fisted boxer' of them all.

Wilde returned to Milwaukee on 29 January to meet the American-Austrian Mike Ertle, whose brother, Johnny 'Kewpie' Ertle, was also a boxer. Jimmy Wilde knocked Ertle out in three rounds, expanding his reputation with American boxing fans.

The next contest was against Mickey Russell on 19 February, at the 4th Regiment Armoury, Jersey City. Russell received a tremendous reception from those who had turned out in the icy weather.

The following table says it all, when comparing the two boxers.

Without much fuss ably, Wilde disposed of Mickey Russell in seven rounds. Relieved the fight was over, he continued to train with sparring partners Al Thompson, Ted Jamieson and Young Dennis (Bow). With every passing day, Jimmy was understanding American boxing a little better: the undeniable opportunities as well as the often illogical decisions of referees when a contest was close and they were awarding points. In a match between Young Dennis and Billy Whelan of St Paul, Billy gave Young Dennis eight of the ten rounds, and yet Young Dennis was denied the decision and lost.

Jimmy's next port of call was Philadelphia to fight Patsy Wallace on 3 March. Jimmy was impressed with Philadelphia, and the City Hall, in particular, stayed in his mind for the rest of his life. The National Athletic Club was packed, with many spectators wishing to see the Mighty Atom. The crowd was split roughly down the middle, although Patsy had some particularly vociferous admirers. One bellowed loud enough for everyone to hear: 'Go in and eat 'um up, Patsy! Go in and eat 'um!'

Jimmy simply smiled, though, as a Calvinist, Elizabeth was displeased. Afterwards, he had plenty of reason to remember the six-round contest. Water on the floor of the dressing room had soaked the soles of his boxing shoes. He had no option but to fight in them, with the consequence that 'sawdust stuck on them like gritty snow', to borrow Jimmy's vivid description. The wet soles hindered his usual boxing style of moving round the ring. To complicate matters further, in the fourth round his glove split. Jimmy could do nothing, for there was not a spare pair available anywhere. David Hughes was furious. Jimmy had to carry on boxing with his right thumb sticking through the glove. He had to be careful, as he did not want to hurt his hand and be out of action for months. He must have looked a pathetic sight with sodden shoes and a badly split glove.

Despite this, Jimmy was determined to get the better of Wallace, and, in the sixth round, he began to throw world-beating punches. Halfway through one of those punches, the damp sawdust sent him slithering like a cork. At the very moment Wallace landed a gentle right on him, Jimmy Wilde was on the floor. Wallace's loyal supporters thought he had knocked the Mighty Atom off his feet.

It was a disaster of a contest, which Jimmy eventually won: a return fight was on the cards. For the press and his large circle of supporters, Patsy Wallace was on the verge of victory.

Jimmy was extremely pleased to have the company of a few Welsh enthusiasts who had come to his dressing room. There were two Welsh supporters from Aberdare as well as the English music hall tenor Talbot O'Farrell. Another interesting supporter present was the popular music hall entertainer Wilkie Bard, who after the war had returned to Broadway with several new characters. One was a Welsh miner based, as some commentators claimed, on none other than Jimmy Wilde. The sketch had been a huge success in London but it did not go down so well with the New Yorkers. The real Jimmy Wilde was their star, not Bard's caricature.

The day after the contest, the promoters offered Wilde a return match with Patsy Wallace, but first he had to travel to Ohio to fight Frankie Mason of Fort Wayne in Toledo on 11 March, eight days away.

Born Frank Edward McCann, Mason was born in Richmond, Indiana, and had fought some of the best fighters, such as Young Zulu Kid and Pete 'King' Herman.

He was roughly the same weight as Jimmy, weighing in at 107 pounds, compared to the Welshman's 106 pounds. The following table from Wilde's book *Fighting was My Business* says it all:

	Mason	**Wilde**
Age:	30 years	28 years
Weight:	107 lbs	106 lbs
Height:	5ft 2½ ins	5ft 2½ ins
Reach:	65¼ ins	68 ins
Chest (normal):	30¾ ins	32½ ins
Chest (expanded):	36 ins	34½ ins
Neck:	13¾ ins	12¾ ins
Thigh:	16½ ins	15½ ins
Waist:	26 ins	22 ins
Calf:	11½ ins	10¼ ins

Ankle:	8¼ ins	8¼ ins
Biceps	11 ins	10¾ ins
Forearm:	10¼ ins	6½ ins
Wrist:	10¾ ins	6¾ ins

In terms of physique, there was little to distinguish the two men, a state of affairs which rarely happened to Wilde. David Hughes was worried who would be the referee. The promoter Addison Q. Thatcher was a tough, rough diamond of a man, and he took David's list of four acceptable referees to the Toledo Boxing Commission. Thatcher warned them the commission was unlikely to be swayed from their own choice, a local referee called Ollie Pecord, who had been in charge of the Dempsey–Willard heavyweight bout in 1919. Pecord had been refereeing since 1898 and was well respected.

Wilde and Hughes had nothing against him, but David Hughes calmly told the commission the referee must be chosen from his own preferred list. They argued for five hours until finally they came to an agreement. The contest would be refereed by Ed Smith of the *Chicago American* newspaper. Smith was by no means an enthusiastic Wilde fan; he had been half-hearted in his summing up of the Wilde–Sharkey contest. Indeed, he thought Mason was the better of the two boxers, and he hoped Mason would take the title from Wilde.

Jimmy had a pleasant surprise when over six hundred Milwaukee enthusiasts, many of them Celts, travelled three hundred miles to support him. He was as popular in Milwaukee as he was in Ferndale, Tylorstown and Pont-y-gwaith in the Rhondda Fach. A few hours before the fight, some Mason fans brought along a cake for the Welsh camp. Jimmy, as a respectable Welsh lad, faced a dilemma. He didn't want to turn the offer down, but he was nervous given his previous bad experience. In the end, they refused the cake, and the Mason camp took it in their stride.

Elizabeth had a difficult night at the ringside. Some over-zealous Mason fans started pulling her hair, tapping her chapel hat forward and making insulting remarks about 'the wizard', which naturally upset her as no one compared to her Jimmy. The situation changed with the arrival of Captain Higgins, the largerthan-life policeman who had previously seconded Freddy Welsh. Captain Higgins was a breath of fresh air and would not allow any unneeded nonsense. Jimmy knew that Mason was a master of clinching; however, the wizard was well prepared. The first five rounds provided exciting boxing, but in the sixth, during a quiet spell, a voice shouted from the ringside in the Welsh language (a language that Jimmy and his team understood and several of them spoke):

> Os wna wnei di orffen ef, Jim, mi ddof i a gwneud hynny fy hunan. Maen nhw'n rhoddi uffern o amser i mi yn y fan hon.

> (If you don't finish him, Jimmy, I'll come and do it myself. They're giving me a hell of a time here!)

Jimmy had a good idea of what the Welsh-speaking spectator had said, and the words inspired him no end. From round six to the end, Mason lost every round. Jimmy aimed to dispatch him in round eleven by a right to the chin, but mistimed it. It was a glaring mistake and the gong sounded. In round twelve, Frankie Mason again went for clinching. Cautioned severely by the referee, he would not listen. He wanted to finish the contest and to survive the ordeal. This he did, but the popular verdict was given, and Ed Smith wrote the next day: 'The reason why Mason was there in the ring when the match was ended was because he could run faster!'

Jimmy was upset with Ed Smith's remarks, but they were in line with the reporter's similar unfair assessment about the Welshman after the Sharkey bout. In fact, the claimant to the flyweight title, Frankie Mason, had received a great deal of manhandling over twelve rounds.

Jimmy and his team had five weeks in which to prepare for their trip to Canada to meet an old friend in the person of Zulu Kid. Jimmy chose to prepare by fighting a number of contests. The first of these was on 21 April at the Sportsman's Club at Camden, New Jersey, against Battling Al Murray, another Italian-American who had been brought up in Philadelphia. The fight in Camden attracted nine thousand spectators. In 1920, the Sportsman's Club was well ahead of its time and imposed a 'no smoking' rule, which was well maintained. It was the first time Jimmy Wilde had fought in a clean atmosphere, except for his open-air fights, and he was thrilled. It wasn't until he began to fight that he realised Battling Al Murray was vicious and dangerous. A hard left to the chin took him by surprise and he found himself on the floor, disappointed and dazed. It was a nasty reminder that he had to be on his guard, for the blow had made him groggy, as his second quickly realised.

Battling Al Murray decided to box at long range, which was a lifeline to the Tylorstown Terror. In fact, Murray could easily have won in the second round by another hard left to the chin. Round three saw Wilde fully recovered, and able to master the rushing bull. One or two of Murray's punches reminded Wilde he was up against a dangerous foe. The crowd was very much for Murray, which upset the Welsh 'wizard' a little.

From that point on, Battling Al Murray found himself on the receiving end of some fierce left hooks. Wilde took him all over the ring, and, on more than one occasion, he was sent reeling onto the ropes. Murray's face was badly swollen, and the referee William H. (Billy) Rocap (1861–1928) and John Smith, the club's chairman, had no option but to stop the fight after Murray landed on the canvas three times in quick succession.

Rocap had been the first amateur bantamweight boxing champion of America in 1888 and 1889. He went on to become a top-class referee, and was in charge of many fights between 1896 and 1921. He refereed

Joe Gans, whom Wilde defeated, Jack Johnson, Pete (Kid) Herman, another of the Welshman's opponents, and Kid Williams.

The contest between Jimmy Wilde and Battling Al Murray was another technical knockout, and the Welsh camp was pleased with the referee's verdict and the outcome. Of the nine fights lined up in the States, eight of them had seen Wilde come out on top, and the only disappointment had been the Sharkey contest. Jimmy was on top of the world, but he was conscious that the Murray fight could have gone the other way. The other boxer could have knocked him out in that first round, and then all the victories would have been nothing as far as the pundits were concerned.

Jimmy knew that Battling Al Murray would be asking for a rematch soon. In the meantime, he was due to meet Bobby Dyson on May Day at the Sportsman's Club, in Lawrence, Massachusetts.

Life in the States was proving both pleasant and unpleasant for the Welsh contingent. They were invited to Freddie Welsh's health farm, in the hamlet of Orangeburg, Orangetown, Rockland County, New York. It was a pleasant place and they were well entertained there. Fred Dyer, the Welsh singer, on a tour of the States, came along to meet them, as did Gus Wilson, who had trained the world-class boxers Jack Dempsey and Georges Carpentier. Freddie Welsh was glad to see Jimmy, but sadly it was their last time together, for Welsh died a few years later, aged 41.

When they returned to their flat in Jersey City, Jimmy and Elizabeth were staggered and annoyed to discover burglars had broken in during their absence and had stripped the place bare. All the silver Jimmy had collected from his tour as prizes had gone forever. The couple took their misfortune in good stride. Another wonderful evening was when they visited Sir David Llewellyn's suite at the Baltimore Hotel, New York. There they met Sybil Vane, the Cardiff singer, while Talbot O'Farrell came along to wish Jimmy well in his forthcoming match against Bobby Dyson.

Wilde was expected to spend the run-up to the contest in Lawrence, Nassau County, where he spent three days attending numerous functions. The fight purse was $8,000, and he earned an additional $500 from film company photoshoots.

On 1 May, Dyson proved no match for Wilde, and he was knocked out in round one, which was not much help for the film company!

The return match with Battling Al Murray was in Philadelphia on 13 May at the National Athletic Club. It was to be an eighteen round contest, which would stretch the energy of both boxers. Murray was, in every way, a tornado of a boxer, and everyone expected him to give Jimmy a hard contest. It did not happen. On the day, Jimmy knocked Murray cold in two rounds.

Jimmy Wilde's USA tour was coming to an end, but he still had to travel to Toronto, Canada, to meet Patsy Wallace for the lineal flyweight title on 24 May. Their rematch took place at the City Hall, the world-famous building in a city which had a sizeable Welsh community. Jimmy was prepared for the controversial fight it turned out to be. In the early rounds, Wallace caught him on the upper lip, cutting it badly (it was later discovered that an artery had been severed). The blood kept pouring out of his mouth, soaking his chin and chest, and even his fighting gear. The seconds did their best, but they were unable to stem the flow. Jimmy looked a poor sight and boxed carefully for the next two rounds, until the bleeding at last stopped. The fight went the whole ten rounds, with the 'no decision' terms, but the general verdict was that Jimmy had retained his title.

Unfortunately, the sports editors of the Toronto newspapers disagreed, as did two veteran North American boxing writers, Bat Masterton of New York's *Morning Telegraph* and William Rocap of the *Public Ledger*, Toronto. Both men were at the ringside and were not fans of Wilde. According to their reports, the referee gave the decision to Wallace by dropping the Union Jack about him at the close of the bout. Then, when referee Lew Marsh was threatened by Wilde's supporters at the ringside, he took the flag off the American and threw it over the blood-covered Wilde. A cordon of police had to escort the referee from the ring.

In its account of the fight, *The Globe* reported that Jimmy Wilde was given a huge shock and a battering. At the end of the third round, Wallace landed two hard rights to Wilde's jaw just as the bell rang. Wilde was dazed and only saved by the bell. In the fourth round, his glove needed changing and, after less than a minute, Lew Marsh stepped in between them and ordered a new glove. The rest gave the Welshman a chance to recuperate. In The Globe's opinion, Wallace had been 'robbed' of the decision.

For *The Mail and Empire*, a crowd of twenty-one thousand saw Wallace in fine form at the end of the ten rounds, while Wilde was in a pitiful condition. *The Toronto Daily Telegraph* maintained that there was huge sympathy for Wilde among the large audience, and that is what kept him going. He had his lip out, and his nose continued bleeding from the fourth round. The Welshman was a sorry sight.

To the sporting columnist and gambler Bat Masterton, both boxers had been handicapped by some new rules which had to be introduced, and it seemed to him that Wilde should not have been allowed to carry on with all the loss of blood.

William Rocap was furious and had been hurt by the Wilde's camp refusal to back him as a possible referee. This time, he claimed Wilde's seconds had deliberated inserted a cut in Jimmy's gloves. The same trick had taken place in Philadelphia five years earlier when Kid Williams, bantamweight champion of the world, fought Johnny Hughes, the European champion. He was on the verge of a knockout when his glove was opened by a penknife. The referee stopped the fight and Hughes was saved from being knocked out.

It seems that all this was sour grapes on the part of Toronto's press, and the referee had mistakenly placed the flag over Wallace when he intended to place it on the world champion. Jimmy Wilde never mentions the rumpus in Toronto. He was simply pleased he had won and his team was on its way home to Wales.

His American trip had been a wonderful success, and there were plenty of offers for him to remain in the States if he cared to prolong his visit. However, he had already heard that a record purse was awaiting him in London, for a contest at the Royal Albert Hall. His opponent would be Pete Herman and they would be fighting for the bantamweight championship of the world.

After leaving Toronto, the Welsh team returned to New Jersey. Wilde was sorry to be leaving and yet he longed for the valleys of Wales. Frankie Burns and his wife were with them, and Peter Donelly a true friend to Jimmy and Elizabeth. He did not want to stay in the States to fight the same men over and over again.

Sammy Harris, a boxing promoter from Baltimore, cabled Jimmy Wilde in early September 1920 with an offer of $7,500 for him to meet Frankie Mason a second time. This time, the contest would be in Baltimore: a twenty-round contest for the flyweight championship of the world.

Jimmy turned it down, for he had beaten Mason decisively, and the offer was nothing to compare with the offer Jack Dempsey's manager Jack Kearns had received for his star to fight Georges Carpentier. That purse was not $7,500 dollars but $175,000!

Jimmy believed Harris should be thinking along those terms. The French boxer Eugène Criqui, had he defeated Walter Ross at Holborn Stadium on 18 September 1919, would also have liked to meet Jimmy Wilde.

He returned a hero and was greeted by many fans at Southampton, including the boxer and trainer John Mortimer. Jimmy and Elizabeth frequently enjoyed weekends with Mortimer and his wife at their Southampton home.

National pride was running high; Wales had produced a great prime minister in David Lloyd George and a great boxer in Jimmy Wilde. Jimmy might not be as outstanding as he'd been in the days he fought Joe Symonds, but he had achieved an excellent record on his tour. For that, he received as much admiration and enthusiasm in south Wales as the statesman.

Financially, he had done well too. He was £23,000 richer as a result of his 1919–20 tour of the USA and Canada.

Gareth Williams, in his study of the boxer, maintains Jimmy Wilde should have announced his retirement after arriving back from Canada and the States. In fact, The Cambrian Daily Leader reported how Jimmy Wilde had announced his decision to retire after fulfilling all his contracts and important contests in the USA. Wilde's love of money prevailed though, and he decided to hold on until he met Herman.

There was no doubt Wilde's trip had raised his profile in the States though. He was praised in the Welsh American press on his visits to New York, New Jersey, Pennsylvania, Ohio and Canada. The Welsh paper Y Drych (The Mirror) placed him on a pedestal, citing Jimmy Wilde as an example to young men everywhere. Earlier in the century, in 1901 and 1905, they had been similarly praising the miners' leader Mabon as an example of a great Welshman.

Jimmy Wilde was getting almost as reverential a treatment, although it would be difficult to outclass Mabon in the eyes of the American Welsh.

The Welsh-language weekly newspaper Tarian y Gweithiwr (The Shield of the Worker) published a poem dedicated to Wilde. Written by a Cardiff teacher, the poem took the form of an englyn, a complex Welsh poem written in strict metre. Edgar Phillips (his bardic name was Trefin after his hometown in Pembrokeshire) would go on to become an Archdruid of the National Eisteddfod of Wales in 1960 until his death. Trefin composed these lines for Jimmy:

> *Dyrnwr â threm byd arno – yw y 'Gwyllt',*
>
> *Gwychaf gawr y cwffio,*
>
> *Od yw'n fach – edwyn efo*
>
> *Fawr dalent hefo'r dwylo.*

The paper's poetry editor Henry Lloyd (bardic name, Ap Hefin) was from Aberdare and said the poem as an excellent tribute to a Welsh sports idol. In it, Edgar Phillips describes Jimmy's craft as well as his physical appearance: he might be small, but he has huge talent in his hands and is a giant in the field of boxing.

To my knowledge, Trefin was the only Welsh poet to honour Jimmy Wilde in this way; however, the *englyn* reveals Jimmy was a hero to young and old, rich and poor, poets and sports editors, politicians and preachers. Indeed, boxing had never been so popular. Every mining town in Britain had a boxing venue and ring. Even small towns could sustain seven to nine professional boxing promotions a month by 1919, and this remained the case until the Second World War.

At the end of 1919, Jimmy's grandmother Catherine Ann Evans was discovered dead at the side of the road just outside Port Talbot. She was 68 years of age. Regrettably, the Wilde family was in New Jersey at the time of her death and so Jimmy missed her funeral. It was a difficult time for him.

CHAPTER 13

WILDE AND THE HERMAN CONTEST

Everything was at first rosy when Jimmy Wilde and his team arrived home in the Rhondda. Jimmy could have easily settled down to a life in the States, as many miners from the Rhondda had been doing since the 1870s.

In Milwaukee, there had been a large German population and, as someone who had served in the army himself and knew the struggle British soldiers had had in defeating the Germans, Jimmy struggled to keep his feelings to himself. Among the six hundred fans who journeyed from Milwaukee to Toledo to support Mason, there must have been two hundred Germans among them. The German immigrants were well treated, and the Americans showed no signs of ill will towards them, as was the case in Liverpool and even in the university town of Aberystwyth on the Cardiganshire coast. In America, it didn't seem to matter what nationality a person had before taking on American nationality. From then onwards, it would always be America first and Germany second. In fact, the boxing community was especially proud of its Italian-American and German-American boxers.

Wilde could not understand why Pete Herman had refused to fight him in the States. Then, out of the blue, came a cable from Rube Welch, offering him a fight with Herman on 13 January 1921. Jimmy hadn't been in the ring since his match with Patsy Wallace. If he could beat the American, it would mean gaining two world titles, which in turn would lead to more lucrative engagements. The promoters were Welch and Pollock who were not only inexperienced, to put it mildly, but also extremely optimistic. They were paying Wilde £8,000, a higher figure than the £6,000 which was being paid to Herman. In addition, they had arranged for the colourful Battling Levinsky, the world lightweight champion, to come to the Albert Hall in London to do battle with Bombardier Billy Wells. All in all, it was a risky venture. Their greatest blunder lay in the manner in which Herman's services were engaged. His contract read that he should defend his bantamweight title against Wilde, and that he should weigh in at two o'clock in the afternoon on the day of the contest. Wilde's agreement, however, stipulated that both he and Herman should weigh eight stone, six pounds at ringside, a totally different stipulation altogether. Having received a substantial advance, the American Herman then purposely tricked both the promoters and his Welsh opponent by losing his world championship to Joe Lynch a week before he set sail for London.

This was unforgiveable, for it meant that Jimmy Wilde could not possibly win the bantamweight championship of the world, and it also gave the deceitful Herman a blatant excuse for coming in at one-and-a-half pounds' overweight. Wilde, who of course was anything up to a stone lighter, strongly objected, and demanded that Herman should weigh in again at ringside. Herman and his manager refused to do this, leaving matters in a delicate position – in fact, a deadlock – right up to the last minute before the boxers entered the boxing ring.

For a reason that was never fully explained to boxing writers or historians, Levinsky withdrew from his bout with Wells. Born Barney Lebrowitz (1891–1949), Levinsky was a Philadelphian lad and began his fighting career as Barney Williams. When Dan Morgan became his manager in 1913, he began calling him Battling Levinsky, the name by which the boxer was known from 1913 to 1920, and with which he won the world light heavyweight championship in 1916 (retaining it until 1920).

Now Levinsky was claiming he had injured his arm and was unable to step into the ring against Wells. There was the possibility a similar fate could befall the Wilde–Herman match. Such an outcome would certainly disappoint the management at the Royal Albert Hall, where the Welsh nation had held their National Eisteddfod over a decade earlier. Worse, it could have led to unprecedented rioting as the miners of Tylorstown and Ferndale, who had journeyed to the famous venue, would not be pleased. Fortunately, the fight went ahead as planned. It was a night that attracted everyone, from fashionable Londoners to the faithful miners who filled the three shillings ten pence seats.

With the start of the fight imminent, Wilde was still in his dressing room, adamant that Herman should make the weight they had agreed on before they entered the ring. The American was equally determined to do nothing of the kind. The situation was growing more desperate by the minute, until an official told Jimmy his great admirer the Prince of Wales was at the ringside waiting for his appearance. That was enough for Wilde. He could not let the prince or his country down; both had been so proud of him over the years. Without any more argument, he told the promoters to inform Pete Herman he was ready to fight. With the light of battle in his eyes and a grim expression on his face, the little Welshman who had taken the world by storm walked out to meet his destiny.

Putting his distinct disadvantage in weight and other physical aspects aside, Jimmy appeared a shadow of his former self that night. Without any warning, he seemed suddenly old, tired and fed up with the world of boxing. It seemed that the long years of the boxing booths, his marvelous career as a professional in Pontypridd, Tonypandy, Liverpool and London, had at last caught up with him. During his tour of North America, there were occasional signs that Jimmy was not as confident of his abilities as he used to be. It seemed the amazing stock of stamina and strength that made him both a fine miner and a superb boxer with the ability to dispose of so many fighters with a knockout had been stolen from him. In the Albert Hall that night, Jimmy Wilde appeared a small, ghost-like figure.

Jimmy understood he had an uphill task to finish a twenty-round contest. In Herman, he was facing a superlative boxer, a man who employed the upstanding British style and whose footwork and use of the straight left delighted his spectators. Wilde was punished by Herman almost from the start, while Herman gave a classic performance that evening. How he would have fared had he been on a par with Wilde with regard to weight, or had met the Tylorstown Terror when he was at peak form, remains a matter of conjecture for the boxing historian. But without doubt, Herman proved himself to be a clever world-beater and certainly he mastered the extraordinary Jimmy Wilde that January evening.

Wilde, the man of courage, kept at it with all his might until the seventeenth round, when his own body rebelled against his spirit and the world-class fighter collapsed in a heap. He looked weary to the boxing commentators when he came out from his corner – indeed, he looked somewhat frightened.

Herman realised Wilde was in a desperate plight and he stepped in remorselessly. Shooting his left through Wilde's guard, he crossed a heavy right to the jaw that sent the Welshman through the ropes to strike his head on the edge of the ring platform. The brave Wilde rose, half-dazed, at the count of seven, and, in a halfcrunched position, tried to reach the centre of the ring. The American was swiftly upon him. A left straightened him up; two rights followed and the world champion was humiliated again as he went through the ropes. This time, he was on his feet inside four seconds; however, he was soon down again, having received a shower of murderous punches.

The hard-hitting New Yorker had badly beaten Wilde. He was hurt all over. Wilde, refusing to give in, distained taking a count, but everyone inside the vast Royal Albert Hall knew he had been knocked out three times between the ropes. He was staggering like a drunken man on a Saturday night when the referee Haley caught him round the waist and waved Herman back. Haley carried the little hero to his corner. Herman said afterwards: 'Wilde is a great fighter, and must have been a wonderful fighter years ago.'

Jimmy had done it for the large purse that was dangled before his eyes. It would have been better if the contest had been for ten rounds. Gareth Williams adds:

> Jimmy won a large purse, but while he was spared the total blindness which eventually afflicted Herman, the true cost was severe headaches and memory loss.

Despite his defeat, Jimmy pleased his many loyal fans with a greathearted performance. He was, above all, an entertainer and it is no wonder he loved acting.

In the opinion of most of his contemporaries, that was the end of Jimmy Wilde in the bantamweight division, a division he should have kept out of at the end of such an illustrious career. As well as being beaten by a much more powerful pugilist who was superior to him on the night, it was obvious Wilde the superman was in decline – some would say, gone forever. Peggy Bettinson told him:

> You have been beaten by the greatest bantam of all time. He knows as much about boxing as Jim Driscoll, Packey McFarland and Jim Corbett. It's no disgrace to be beaten by such a perfect master. I must say you're extraordinary to have lasted seventeen rounds with him.

Ted Lewis was heartbroken. He had two concerns: first, he should have called the fight off over the weighing-in affair, and, secondly, he should not have agreed to a contest which lasted over twenty rounds. When they discovered that Wilde was well ahead of Herman on points in the fifteenth round, they were extremely annoyed at their blunder. After the Herman contest, Jimmy heeded Elizabeth's pleadings and his own reasoning, and decided for the second time to call it a day and to enjoy his life on the outskirts of Cardiff, near enough to Tylorstown and the valleys. He had been boxing non-stop for twelve years and now it was time to become a friend to his two sons and to give Elizabeth more of his company and support. He later recalled how the bad concussion he suffered during the Herman fight was the beginning of 'a great deal of pain in the head'.

The inhabitants of Radyr were kind and helpful to Jimmy, and proud he was coming back to live in their community. He did an exhibition fight at Mountain Ash in aid of the south Wales miners during the 1921 strike. Dai Evans, a warm-hearted friend, organised the event and Jimmy felt at home with a real Welsh welcome at the ringside. Ernie Robinson from the village of Cwm, near Ebbw Vale, was the first boxer to spar with him. Another Monmouthshire boxer, Billy Jones of Ynysddu, did well in the second exhibition contest. The miners were thrilled, as were Jimmy and Dai Evans when they announced £184 was to be sent to the strikers' fund. Jimmy also announced that the money raised from selling his gloves, for the sum of 12 pounds and 10 shillings (or nearly £200 today), was to be added to a cause that meant so much to him, namely helping his mining friends in their time of need.

CHAPTER 14

A SAD END TO A GLITTERING CAREER

In America, a sensational Filipino boxer named Francisco 'Pancho Villa' Guilledo had burst onto the scene. Guilledo is considered by many to be the greatest Asian fighter in boxing history. Just over five-foot-tall, Villa was explosive and dangerous for any opponent. Born Francisco Guilledo on the island of Panay in the Philippines, his reputation brought him to the attention of promoter Frank Churchill in Manila. Impressed with Guilledo, Churchill began to manage him, naming him after the famous Mexican bandit Pancho Villa.

In 1922, Churchill brought Villa to the United States, where he won the flyweight championship of America by knocking out Johnny Buff. Their enthusiasm fuelled by the win, Villa's backers wanted to give him the chance to become world champion. Jimmy Wilde had held the crown since 1916, and so overtures were made to Ted Lewis and Jimmy was invited to the States to defend his title. Elizabeth was against the idea, and she and Ted discussed the invitation at length. The purse to fight Villa was £13,000, a huge amount to the Welsh team. In the end, the temptation for Jimmy Wilde to fight Pancho Villa proved too great.

It was a blunder of the first order. Jimmy had not fought, except against Herman, for two and a half years. For his final fight, he was choosing a boxer he knew little about. It was Jimmy Wilde who had made flyweight boxers popular with the public. As Ed Hughes of *The Brooklyn Daily Eagle* said of him in 1920: 'Jimmy Wilde is one of the "immortals" of Queensberry. Probably you'll never see his like again.'

Wilde possessed all the attributes needed to become 'immortal'. Above all, he had a terrific punch. Frankie Mason, Johnny Buff, Frankie Genaro, Fidel LaBarba, Isadore 'Corporal Izzy' Schwartz, Newsboy Brown: few boxers in the flyweight division had been noted for their punches until Wilde stepped into the ring.

Wilde travelled to New York with Elizabeth and Ted Lewis. He displayed no lack of confidence during his preparations for the contest. Most of his friends thought Jimmy was making a grave error, and tempting his physical welfare by making a comeback. During his lengthy lay-off, he'd spent more time playing golf and billiards than boxing training.

The contest against Pancho Villa was scheduled for 16 June 1923 at the Polo Grounds, New York. Wilde was ten years older than Villa, and had no hope of escaping from the Filipino and his vicious punching and fast non-stop attacking. But Wilde, who had always displayed tons of confidence and self-will throughout his remarkable boxing career, was as confident as he could be. He was fully determined to battle to the last in order to preserve his title and his reputation. The fight against Guilledo might be his last, but if he was going to be beaten, he was going to go to the floor with the Welsh dragon flying high and the spirit of Owain Glyndŵr racing proudly through his veins.

Twenty-three thousand people gathered at the Polo Grounds on a beautiful night to witness the epic battle, which deserves to be described in detail.

Round One

Both boxers emerge from their corners in a flash determined to fight. They begin mixing it in the centre of the ring. The spectators witness excellent defence on both sides, and a great deal of snappy and brilliant footwork. The Filipino lands a left to Wilde's head, but it's a light blow. They exchange left punches, which leads to a clinch.

They're hammering each other all over the stomach. Villa is tearing punches to the body and then to the head, as if he is on a crusade. Clinch again. Referee Patsy Haley has a huge job on his hands. He breaks them apart again, and feels frustrated as he has to do it so often.

Gong

That's Round One over. From the first moment, it was obvious the Welshman was painfully slow and had lost his old-time fighting zeal and boxing might. The dark-skinned Villa tore into him like a bull, his flashing gloves beating a tattoo on Wilde's head.

Gong Round Two

They are out for Round Two and immediately into the centre of the ring. *Ow ow ow!* Villa pastes a hard-right punch to Jimmy's jaw, and he is in a dizzy state. He goes into a clinch for a breather, holding on, and the Filipino is attacking his body in a savage manner. He's got Wilde groggy! The great champion is staggering around the ring! Villa is throwing everything at him – everything but plates from the kitchen! Villa is walloping him all around the ring to the disappointment of the world champion. Wilde comes in for a clinch again. Haley intervenes and breaks them apart, but the champion is struggling. This looks like the end. Wilde is trying his very best to come back, to defend himself until the end of the second round. He needs a dose of smelling salts.

The last swing by Pancho Villa Lands Jimmy Wilde on the mat, and his seconds come out and carry him back to his corner. They want to work on him, so he can face Round Three. Villa staggered Wilde with a right and had him on the verge of a knockout defeat. With amazing gameness, Jimmy refused to go down and he will fight on for a few more rounds. Villa had delivered a foul blow, even if it was unintentional, and the referee foolishly ruled that the contest should proceed.

Gong Round Three

Jimmy staggers on to his feet and Villa goes three quarters of the way to meet him. Jimmy has no option but to try and fight. But he's truly beaten. The Filipino is in complete control and is waiting confidently for his moment of glory. He is so relaxed, so confident, and tires Jimmy with every punch.

Gong

Jimmy came out to take another fearful hammering, and the blood is pouring out of the cuts. It is only a question of time.

Gong Round Four

Within a second, the two marvelous boxers, the best the world had seen until that point, are slugging it away as well as entertaining the large number of spectators. Jimmy is worn out and has no more energy left, and Pancho Villa is able to face all his boxing attacks.

Gong

The referee ruled that the contest should proceed as Jimmy didn't want to throw in the towel.

Gong Round Five

Both men are obviously tired. Villa lands a left to the stomach that doubles Jimmy up. It hurts him, and Villa lands a hard left to the face of the brave Welshman.

Gong

Both men returned to their corners. Jimmy's eye was shut and his face plastered with blood. Villa was mostly unmarked. Jimmy showed extreme courage, and the seconds did an excellent job on his battered face.

Gong Round Six

Villa immediately lands lefts and rights to Jimmy's body. The

Filipino lands a left to his face, and Jimmy staggers back towards the corner! Villa is after his prey. The Welshman is under a hail of fists: to his nose, lips, eyes, chin, chest, stomach, even the back of his head. Wilde is staggering under such an attack. It's all over. Surely, he can't stand much more? But he is stubborn and refuses to fall onto the mat. Villa is beating him with both fists, but the Mighty Atom will not surrender. Wilde is stooping over with his arms wrapped around his head. He is incredible in the face of his inevitable defeat, and he is still on his feet, unsteady, determined, and displaying the grit of the Rhondda miners.

Gong

What a round! The crowd was shouting for the referee to stop the contest, saying Jimmy Wilde didn't deserve such punishment so far from home. Ted Lewis and Wilde's seconds begged their hero to toss in the towel, but he refused. He had never, never surrendered to anyone in his life. His seconds scraped the blood from his body and face, from his nose, from a gash on his cheek, from his closed eye and another cut over his eye. Wilde's eyes were almost closed and soon he wouldn't be able to see anything. The time had come for him to retire.

Gong Round Seven

Both eyes are closing and Jimmy Wilde is bleeding from several cuts. He can barely raise his arms to defend himself, but Villa has no sympathy; his only wish is to destroy the champion. Rights and lefts, Wilde is like a top. He moves from pillar to post, reeling as he does all over the ring. Taking terrible punishment, but too stubborn to give in, his strong arms are letting him down. He is no longer able to defend himself. Then it comes: a rigid inside swing to the jaw. Jimmy Wilde is on the mat. He is down. Patsy Haley is counting one to ten above the body of the greatest boxing champion Wales has ever produced. There are tears in the referee's eyes. The wonder-man has been pulped and badly beaten, not in front of the loyal miners of the Rhondda, but before lovers of boxing from every nation under the sun. He had done a huge mistake and it was sad that he would be returning to Wales a badly beaten boxer. The crown fell to the floor with him It was a pathetic sight, and the distinguished boxing writer J. C. Kofoed of The Orlando Sentinel maintained it was the 'saddest sight I ever saw in the ring'. He explains why he felt that way:

> Wilde was probably the greatest little man that ever lived. Though he scarcely weighed more than a hundred pounds, he had the greatest knock-out recorded in the flyweight class, often defeating men weighing twenty pounds more than him.

To Kofoed, Jimmy was not knocked out. Rather, he collapsed, still moving forward and pawing at his foe. He went down as the tradition of the ring demands the champion goes, the tradition founded on the same theory that makes a captain stick to his ship when it is sinking in the might of the waves and the storm. He stays there a victor in defeat.

Kofoed spoke to Jimmy the following day. The boxer had no recollection of the final blow that sent him to the floor, a short right hook to the jaw. No boxer ever fought with more courage than Jimmy Wilde did that night, and no champion ever suffered a worse beating in the last desperate defence of his title. Pancho Villa had everything to win and nothing to lose. He threw caution to the wind and weakened Wilde with body blows, making him easy prey as the battle wore on. One must also remember that Villa's blow to the back of Jimmy's head would have seen him disqualified in the United Kingdom; in the States, it only earned him a pathetic warning from the referee. Forty thousand people turned out to see Jimmy Wilde once more, and Elizabeth left her seat in the fifth round to walk to his dressing room. There, she waited for the ultimate defeat.

In Elizabeth's words, Jimmy looked like 'a mass of pulp' when he was carried to his dressing room unconscious. As always, his team rallied around him. Benny Williams applied ice to Jimmy's face and spine with tears in his eyes, while Tom O'Rourke, the manager who had brought him here, went in search of a doctor. By far the most moving moment was when Pancho Villa came to Jimmy's dressing room himself and asked in broken English: 'How, how you feel, Jimmy?' Then he turned to Elizabeth and told her: 'Me no want to hurt him. Not me do that.'

Poor Villa. He gained very bad publicity for the foul blow that should have disqualified him. Tragically, just two years later, he died from complications from a tooth extraction; he was 23.

The Phillipines boxing tradition received a huge boost from Pancho Villa's fight with Jimmy Wilde and his subsequent world title. Today the country is a proud fighting nation which has produced forty-two world champions.

Jimmy remained in a coma for eight hours. At one point in the early hours, Dr Louis Draper, who was treating him, was concerned the boxer would never see the mining valleys of Wales again.

Jimmy remained unconscious while an exhausted Dr. Draper relieved the pressure from the neck. As he explained to Elizabeth, the punches had 'jammed the neck and fascial muscles, temporarily locked the neck to the spine, and produced a form of neurasthenia'.

Elizabeth obeyed the doctor's orders and applied ice to her husband's face and called out his name in an attempt to rouse him. Thankfully, their combined efforts proved successful and Jimmy lived to see another day.

The once powerful Wilde was severely weakened and needed a great deal of nursing. Elizabeth spoon-fed him with milk and the ice cream Jimmy loved. It took three weeks of loving care and nursing to get him back to his usual confident self. Dr. Draper, Ted Lewis, Benny Williams and, above all, Elizabeth, had been responsible for restoring his good health.

Dr. Draper was able to relieve Jimmy of his discomfort, enabling the Wildes to enjoy some relaxation with friends in New Year. Frankie Burns, the bantamweight champion, and his wife had a bungalow on a small island near New York. To avoid the crowds who were looking out for Jimmy Wilde – to them, he was still the undisputed world champion – they hired a boat to cross the Hudson River. When the boat was within easy distance of the shore, a lightning flash struck two men standing on the small landing stage, killing them instantly. Jimmy and Elizabeth were fortunate to have escaped – this time providence had been kind to them.

Jimmy Wilde's boxing career had been beyond successful but his fighting days were over. An era of wonderful boxing had ended. Sir Alfred Downing Fripp, who was surgeon to both King Edward VII and King George V, offered the boxer this stern warning should he be tempted to enter the ring again: 'You'll kill yourself.'

CHAPTER 15

TIMES OF TRIBULATION

Jimmy took a long time to recover from his fight against Pancho Villa. His life became one tribulation after another throughout the 1920s and 1930s. In 1922, he fell from his horse when out hunting with the Pentyrch hounds in the Vale of Glamorgan and needed again to be nursed to health by Elizabeth.

When he retired, Jimmy believed he was a wealthy man; he had at least £70,000 banked, but he began to squander his hard-earned cash. In his own words:

> I was a comparatively wealthy man; for the first time in my life, I had leisure to enjoy wealth; and I had to be treated like a semi-invalid. The process of recovery was very slow.

His first investment was in a starting-price business in Cardiff. It prospered for a while, but eventually went under, with a net loss of at least £10,000. It was a bitter blow for Jimmy and the beginning of his troubles.

Next, he was offered a stake in cinemas throughout the Rhondda. He bought a few, including the Coliseum Cinema in Tylorstown, where he had appeared on numerous occasions in his heyday. He also bought a number of terraced houses, an investment which also resulted in a considerable loss, for the mining communities were in decline. Between 1921 and 1936, 241 collieries had closed down in South Wales, while the workforce decreased from 271,161 in 1920 to 126,233 in 1936. In the same period, the collieries' wages bill had been reduced from £65 million to £14 million. South Wales was witnessing poverty on a huge scale, and Jimmy Wilde was trying to make money in the Rhondda, of all places.

Then came the 1926 General Strike, followed by the seven months' coal strike, and Jimmy had no choice but to lend his name to the struggle and appear at events to raise money for his fellow miners. He had once been one of them, and remained so at heart; Jimmy admired the Rhondda miners' leaders, notably A. J. Cook, Noah Ablett and Arthur Horner, and, like them, he played a vital role in supporting the miners, including financially. Jimmy's heart bled when the miners and his comrades were starved to surrender.

By 1931, the Rhondda had become a depressed area – but this was the very place where Jimmy had a sizeable amount of his cash invested. There was no alternative industry in the Rhondda to mining, as Jimmy knew better than anyone else. A large number of his generation had left for new pastures. The net decrease in the Rhondda's population in the ten years from 1921 to 1931 was 21,371 – the greatest decrease in the whole of Wales. It has been estimated that between the two World Wars (1919–39), some fifty thousand people left the Rhondda, meaning the area lost a population equal to a city the size of Gloucester. Jimmy and Elizabeth were among them. Their friends were leaving for towns like Slough and Watford, Luton and Oxford, as well as Birmingham and Coventry. The social and psychological consequences of those years of depression have been underlined by the Rhondda historians E. D. Lewis, Dai Smith and Cliff Williams, who highlight the intense human suffering, low standards of living and general lack of social amenities. This, in an area which, over seventy years, had extracted more wealth than any other part of the United Kingdom.

Rhondda communities had produced more world-famous boxers than any valley in the world. In addition to Jimmy Wilde of

Tylorstown, there was Tom Thomas of Pen-y-graig, first holder of the middleweight Lonsdale belt; Freddie Welsh, world lightweight title holder; Percy Jones of Porth, flyweight champion of the world before Wilde; and Llew Edwards of Porth, British featherweight champion. The three venues in Tylorstown, the Judges' Hall, Trealaw, and the Llwynypïa Baths, witnessed many memorable boxing contests.

Despite everything, Jimmy and Elizabeth decided to send their sons David and Verdun to King's College, a public school in Taunton, Somerset. It was a move they could not afford and their decision attracted criticism from Jimmy's fans.

However, it was Jimmy Wilde's association with Jimmy White that lost him most of his hard-earned money. White was a flamboyant character who had loved supporting Jimmy as a boxer. He was full of ideas and colourful entertainment, and used his charm on Jimmy to invest in a production of Katja the Dancer in Daly's Theatre, London. Jimmy foolishly invested over £10,000 in White's scheme.

With hindsight, Jimmy's decision to invest in the production was foolhardy. His friendship with White was a bone of contention between him and Elizabeth. With the business in Cardiff floundering, Elizabeth argued forcefully that he should not put all his eggs in one basket. Jimmy stood his ground.

When White came back asking for more investment in Katja the Dancer, Jimmy went to his safe to look for shares he could sell. Elizabeth was livid.

'Whose money is it, I ask you?' Jimmy demanded.

Elizabeth answered: 'Mine as much as yours. Give me them!'

She was right. In a marriage, all one's wealth is divided between husband and wife.

Jimmy's naivety and gullibility were apparent. For him, White could do no wrong and he refused to give in. After a few months, Elizabeth insisted Jimmy ask his friend for a statement of profit. Treating the matter as urgent, the couple caught a train to Paddington and, for six days in succession, Jimmy attempted to arrange a meeting with Jimmy White. Each time, his secretary gave a different excuse for his absence: he was at a conference, he'd been taken ill, or had just left the office.

On the seventh day, they finally pinned him down. Jimmy explained he needed some of his cash back, a thousand pounds. The seventh day was different. White reverted to type, insisting Katja the Dancer would make them a fortune, but they had to be patient. Jimmy Wilde didn't get his thousand pounds. He asked for it again two months later, and at Elizabeth's insistence. This time, there was no response.

The reason for Jimmy White's silence became apparent in Cardiff a few days later. Wilde had gone to the offices of the starting-price business, where he was surprised to find his wife talking to manager Bill Collins.

'Have you seen the placards?' Elizabeth asked him. Jimmy had not.

'Jimmy White's committed suicide. Do you hear that?'

Wilde was dumbfounded and turned as white as a sheet. He well remembered the other man's self-assurance and confidence, along with his constant talk of making a fortune. The fact was a very sizeable chunk of Wilde's capital was tied up in Katja the Dancer. Elizabeth was furious. She reminded him of her ongoing concerns with the investment, and scolded him for having more faith in his deceiver than in her. Then she got up and marched out, shouting loudly at Jimmy, 'And I'm leaving you!'

For her, the episode was big enough to do that, but Collins ran after her: 'You mustn't talk like that, Mrs. Wilde.'

Elizabeth dealt with her husband in her own way. Before the end of the day, she had asked the secretary Chella to get a hundred pounds from the ailing company, saying she was going to have a wonderful time in London. Hours later, she and Jimmy were in the capital, determined to enjoy every moment there.

Jimmy confessed:

> I think – and others have agreed – that if 'Lisbeth had not acted like that it would have broken me finally. As it is – well, the failure of the S. P. business and the continued slump in the picture-houses – houses did not seem as important as they were, and we kept smiling.

The couple were also heavily involved in the charities of Sir Harry Preston in Brighton. Elizabeth would often sing at the charity events and cheerily entertain a full house. She had no formal training; however, her years spent in the Band of Hope in the Nonconformist chapel were a useful training ground. Whenever they were in Brighton, Sir Harry looked after the couple well, usually providing them with a room at the Royal Albion Hotel. On one occasion, Jimmy travelled from London to Brighton with the circus supremo Bertram Mills, who served as an executive and exhibited a flair for organising charity shows.

Sir Harry Preston enjoyed the patronage of the Prince of Wales for shows held at the Brighton Dome on behalf of the Royal Sussex County Hospital. In addition to entertainers, Jimmy Wilde was able to attract a large number of boxing stars, including

Tommy Burns, Pat O'Keeffe, Dick Smith, Matt Wells, Joe Bowker, Jack Dempsey, Georges Carpentier, Matt Moran and Joe Beckett. Bombardier Billy Wells was another stalwart of these shows. Sir Harry was delighted with Jimmy, who had a way of getting other boxers involved. Jack Dempsey once put off an important meeting at the end of his honeymoon to stay and box at Brighton because he had promised to do so. His delightful wife, the American actress Estelle Taylor, agreed with the change of plans! The Royal Sussex County Hospital is claimed to have benefitted by at least £40,000 from Sir Harry Preston's shows, which provided high-quality entertainment year after year.

In one of the shows, Jimmy fought an exhibition with the French boxer, actor and First World War pilot Georges Carpentier. Carpentier had campaigned in every class from flyweight to heavyweight and was regarded as one of the greatest European fighters to ever lace a pair of gloves. To everyone's surprise, Jimmy proved he could fight a heavyweight champion of Carpentier's calibre and survive – mostly by his unmatched footwork.

Jimmy was known in the boxing world as one of the most generous supporters of charities, especially those linked with children and hospitals. As well as Brighton, he went a number of times to Margate and Harrogate. Sadly, on at least four occasions, thieves broke into the couple's home, including once when Jimmy was in Harrogate exhibiting his Lonsdale belt, a proud possession of his.

That time, they returned home after David contacted them. Of the 150 trophies Jimmy had won, twenty-three of the most precious had been stolen. The thieves even took a cup Verdun had won at a King's College marathon, a loss which particularly upset Elizabeth. The theft of Jimmy's silver trophies was particularly mean because the thieves would have only got the melting price for them. They were never returned, and the theft was all the more deplorable for taking place while Jimmy and Elizabeth were making an effort to help others and make the world a better place.

Another organisation Jimmy supported was the Boy Scouts Association. He'd first become involved after receiving a letter from

Viscount Castlereagh, welcoming his 1938 autobiography and reminding him of his support for the Scouts:

> I remember, year after year, meeting you in Sunderland, at the dinner preceding the Boy Scouts' Boxing Tournament, at which you were the third man in the ring. You came all the long way from Wales of your own free will, and at your own expense. It is hardly necessary to add what an encouragement it was to those splendid boys.

Through the enthusiasm of Horace and Bob Alaway, Jimmy also got himself involved with the amateur football club the Middlesex Wanderers. As president and honorary secretary of the club, the brothers were involved in the club for at least fifty years. When Jimmy met them, he was impressed with their dedication towards amateur football. The Middlesex Wanderers was established primarily to develop a first-class amateur team that could visit countries in Europe and enlarge the horizons of all those associated with the club. The Wanderers achieved a huge deal for charity and established the Richmond Boxing Day Regatta, which became an annual attraction, as did the yearly Sportsman's Service at Finsbury Town Hall. Jimmy spent hours with the Wanderers, inspiring a large number of the lads to get involved in cricket too. Most of the cricket matches were held abroad, and Jimmy and Elizabeth would often join the lads in Germany, Belgium, Denmark and Holland. It was through the Middlesex Wanderers that Jimmy got involved with the Peel Institute, a boys' club which worked with young men from underprivileged backgrounds in the poorer districts of London. The positive influence of prominent sportsmen generally brought the best out of these lads.

Jimmy received a great deal of publicity in 1938 when Boy McCormick, the former light heavyweight boxing champion of Great Britain, claimed damages for alleged libel. The case was heard before Mr. Justice Hawke and a sporting jury in the King's Bench division. The boxer sued in the name of Noel Hugh McCormick of Derby Hotel in Salford. His complaint related to an article that appeared in the Sunday newspaper The People in January 1936 and was reproduced in a book called Giants on Parade. McCormick argued that the offending article, written by B. Bennison, implied he was knocked out by Jimmy Wilde during the First World War. It is true that, in 1917, while both men were serving in the army, he and Jimmy Wilde had faced each other. Rowland Thomas QC represented McCormick and argued that it had been a sparring bout. No one had been damaged, and his client had not been knocked out.

Jimmy Wilde gave evidence. He had weighed six stone eight pounds when the two-round exhibition took place. At the end of the second round, McCormick's father had announced, 'That will do,' before taking his son out of the ring. Edward Barry Dent, licensee of the Prince of Orange public house in Dover, a regimental major and boxing instructor at Aldershot in 1917, described the contest, recalling that Jimmy Wilde had spent most of the time ducking about and making a fool of his opponent. 'McCormick lost his temper and became nasty, and Wilde realised this and got in a blow to the chin that no other British boxer in that time could deliver,' Dent said, adding: 'McCormick stood there like a soldier on parade; he could neither fall backwards or forwards.'

Many of those in the courtroom appreciated Dent's description and smiled at his humour. The boxer's libel case was against The People newspaper, the book's publishers Rich & Cowan Ltd, publisher of Bennison's book, and Richard Clay and Sons, the book's printers. The jury returned a verdict for the plaintiff and awarded him the sum of £750 in respect of the article and £300 for the book, a total of £1,050. It seemed to the boxing fraternity a wrong decision for, if there had been a ring, his father could not have got there in time and the boy would have been down and out, in other words, 'knocked out'.

The interwar years were not kind to Jimmy Wilde. During that time, his life seemed to reflect the depression and unemployment witnessed in the Rhondda. Aneurin Bevan crossed swords with the official Labour Party in south Wales with his suggested scheme for the enrolment of British youth in a movement that would combine boxing, cycling, hiking and mountain climbing. Jimmy Wilde thought Bevan's proposed scheme would counteract the fascism which was taking hold in London as in south Wales. Working-class groups would train, take an oath of allegiance, and not be affiliated to any political party. The scheme was opposed by the moderate miners' leaders and Jimmy Wilde, like Aneurin Bevan, had to swallow the bitter pill of being heavily defeated.

CHAPTER 16

JIMMY AND THE BOXING FRATERNITY

Boxing was a passion for Jimmy Wilde. Indeed, he came from a boxing milieu. When he was the undisputed flyweight champion of the world, his mother got involved in a punch-up on a late October evening. Maggie Wilde emerged from a hotel in Caerphilly (a favourite haunt of the Wilde family), placed her hat on the windowsill and shouted over at Mary Bowen, who was walking in front of her. Mary Bowen was the stronger of the two that evening, and she knocked Maggie Wilde to the floor, continuing to deliver punches. Maggie sustained a broken leg and other injuries. It was an episode Jimmy Wilde would have preferred to forget: two grown women brawling on the floor, and one of them his mother. Unfortunately, we have no idea what triggered the ferocious fight among these two grown up women.

Jimmy was brought up in a Valleys community where boxing was admired by all and there, existed men of huge boxing talent. His own idol was Peerless Jim Driscoll, who was born and brought up in an Irish ghetto in Cardiff. Paul O'Leary has written on the Catholic priests who supported boxing in their parishes. He maintains:

> A number of priests established boxing schools for youngsters in their parishes as a way of instilling in them self-discipline and diverting them from more dangerous activities on the streets. There was never a conflict between religion and boxing, as far as Driscoll was concerned. Both piety and sport were essential ingredients in the distinctive popular culture that he

inherited in his youth and which, in turn, he helped shape as an adult.

Driscoll was more fortunate than Jimmy, as most of the Nonconformist ministers in the Rhondda were unable to see what the Catholic priests in Cardiff saw, which was a huge potential in disciplining tough working-class lads. There were exceptions, but the majority failed to grasp the potential of boxing, as well as the need for socialism as a philosophy to believe in.

Jim Driscoll was a handsome man, and became one of the masters of the noble art of self-defence. Jimmy Wilde became his most famous pupil, and he learnt to appreciate Driscoll's straight left delivered as a scoring punch. He learnt much from him, and also from his apprenticeship in the boxing booths. For it was in the booths that Jimmy learnt to duck and then slip in the damaging punches. To the delight of Jimmy and his family, Driscoll took the British featherweight title from Joe Bowker with a knockout in the seventeenth round on 1 June 1907 at the National Sporting Club in London. He held on to his British crown until he retired in 1913, soon after he had been held to a draw by Owen Moran. From 1913, Jim Driscoll took Jimmy in hand, and his style became that of his teacher, though his methods of attack were always his own.

It is interesting to read Jimmy Wilde's opinion of boxers outside the flyweight and bantamweight division. He had a tremendous admiration for Jack Dempsey, one of the most colourful characters in boxing history. Dempsey's real name was William Harrison and, when he began in the ring, he was as poor as a church mouse. There is an old saying that hungry fighters are the best fighters, and Dempsey knew what hard work was when he began working in the shipyards of Seattle. When his brother died, Harrison returned to the ring because his family needed the money for funeral expenses. A rugged, non-stop fighter, he always made his spectators loyal to his style, and went on to win the heavyweight title from Jess Willard in three rounds at Toledo in Ohio on 4 July 1919. Though he conceded almost four stone to the giant Willard, he proved himself the most superb boxer of all times by flooring the Kansas cowboy seven times in the first round.

Dempsey took another two rounds to defeat the biggest man ever to have held the world title. Willard's trainers then threw in the towel, indicating to the referee that their boxer did not want to carry on fighting. Dempsey had a huge regard for Jimmy Wilde. It was Dempsey who told Jimmy to think of refereeing, which he did for years. However, no one earned as much money as Dempsey did as a referee. The young lad who had earned three dollars and fifty cents for winning his first fight received $10,000 for refereeing the Ceferino Garcia v Glen Lee middleweight bout in 1939.

To Jimmy, there was only one heavyweight champion who was superior to Dempsey in the heavyweight class, and that was Jack Johnson. Wilde had the same opinion of Johnson as the boxing journalist Nat Fleischer did. For Fleischer, Johnson and Jimmy Wilde were in a class of their own. In 1926, Fleischer wrote an interesting article in the Rutland Daily Herald, Vermont, entitled 'Supermen of the Ring'. To him, Johnson and Wilde were the supermen of boxing history. He mentioned Johnson as being the 'best all-round heavyweight' but also as 'the fighter with the best defence, the best upper cut, the best counter-puncher, best at fainting and the most craft' according to boxing historian Maurice Golesworthy.

Jimmy Wilde argued that only Jack Johnson 'was superior to Dempsey in the heavyweight class'. Wilde met Gene Tunney when he was with the Allied Services in England, and they became firm friends. Jimmy was surprised at how unassuming Tunney was. For his part, Tunney believed 'Wilde was the best boxer of all times'. Tunney won the world title by outpointing Jack Dempsey over ten rounds at Philadelphia on 23, September 1926.

He defeated the Manassa Mauler for a second time over the same distance a year later. Tunney, after collecting nearly a $1,750,000 for three world titles, announced his retirement as undefeated champion. Wilde sums him up in a memorable sentence: 'Quiet, reserved, intellectual, he carved a special niche for himself in boxing history.'

So did Primo Carnera, the giant Italian known as the Ambling Alp, who stood at nearly six feet six inches in his socks and weighed around nineteen stone (266 pounds). Carnera was discovered in the circus, and was subsequently brought to London. Jimmy was greatly concerned for the Italian. In his opinion, he was exploited and swindled from start to finish. As a boxer, he won the world heavyweight champion by defeating Jack Sharkey in the sixth round at Madison Square Garden Bowl, Long Island City, on 29 June 1933, having previously lost to him in October 1931. Wilde assesses him in his autobiography:

> Primo Carnera, amiable fellow though he was, had no idea of directing or timing his punches, and still less of making any defensive play. His strength and stamina kept him going where many others would have been knocked out.

Another superb heavyweight that Jimmy admired was Joe Louis After all, from the day Louis won the world heavyweight title by stopping James J. Braddock on 22 June 1937 until he announced his retirement in March 1949, he defended his crown twenty-five times. Wilde himself never achieved such a record and forgets to mention that only three boxers went the distance with him: The Welshman Tommy Farr, Arturo Godoy and Jersey Joe Walcott. Wilde knew Louis had knocked out six world heavyweight champions: Max Schmeling, Jack Sharkey, Primo Carnera, Max Baer, James J Braddock and Jersey Joe Walcott. He has nothing to say about these fighters, though he wondered whether Max Baer took boxing as seriously as he should, and he also mentions the German hero Max

Schmeling, who is remembered for his victory over Louis on 19 June 1936 in New York.

Jimmy Wilde and Tommy Farr are generally exalted as heroes in Welsh boxing, yet it is clear Farr upset Wilde. Jimmy had acted as matchmaker for Farr's first fight in Wimbledon and had high hopes of managing the boxer, one of the best British heavyweights Wales had produced in its boxing history, but the whole project fell through. Jimmy Wilde in his autobiography does not mention how near Tommy Farr came to defeating Joe Louis in August 1937. His remarkable performance in that contest in New York overshadowed everything else he did. Born in Clydach Vale, Rhondda, on 12 March 1913, Farr started boxing as a professional fighter in 1926.

Wilde praises Ben Foord for his performance against Schmeling, but did not mention Farr's contest with Foord, on 11 March 1937, when the Rhondda Fawr fighter was on top form. Farr later outpointed Max Baer at Harringay, and in so doing gave a remarkable performance, one of the most scintillating before the Second World War.

Wilde has thrown his net a long way, and he brings Len Harvey, Joe Beckett, Jack Petersen, Jack Bloomfield, Jack Kid Berg and Peter Kane to our attention, many of them long-forgotten heroes of the ring. Len Harvey was a Cornishman and, like Wilde, was not afraid of fighting. He was never inactive; indeed, he fought 418 contests between 1919 and 1942. When Harvey was at the peak of his career, Jimmy wrote a great deal on him as the boxing correspondent to the News of the World. During his busy boxing life, Len Harvey won three British and Empire titles, namely heavyweight, light heavyweight and middleweight, and he was also named the world light heavyweight champion. Wilde saw him in November 1933 giving one of the best displays of his career, when he caused a great shock to the boxing world by taking the British heavyweight title from Jack Petersen at the Albert Hall.

Wilde met Jack Bloomfield towards the end of World War One while he served in the RAF. Jimmy tipped him then as a likely champion in the near future and encouraged the Islington lad to fight Harry Drake, Ted 'Kid' Lewis and Frank Goddard. Jimmy was present on 9 August 1924 when Bloomfield was knocked out in the third round by Tom Gibbons, the high-ranking Irish American heavyweight.

Jack Petersen was a friend of Jimmy's, and was a huge attraction in all the Welsh and London venues. Like Driscoll, he was born in Cardiff, and his first ambition was to be a doctor, but the lure of the ring proved too much for him. Soon he was a champion, winning the British light heavyweight title, as well as the heavyweight title. His achievement was to make the Lonsdale belt his property, and he had victories over Jack Pettifer and Jack Doyle before losing the title in November 1933 to Len Harvey.

Jimmy regarded Joe Beckett as one of Britain's most underrated boxing champions. He came to the attention of Wilde just before World War One, in the services competitions, where he did well. Jimmy followed his career – including his win over the Canadian Tommy Burns in 1920, when he defeated him in seven rounds – until Beckett's retirement in 1923.

To Wilde, Jack 'Kid' Berg was a fine fighter. He always said that no British boxer did more to uphold the standards of Britain in the boxing rings of America than Berg. An outstanding lightweight of his time, he never achieved greatness. Wilde sums him up well: 'Kid Berg was a fine fighter – if only he had extra in his punches!' By the end of the 1930s, Jimmy Wilde felt that the golden age of boxing had passed. Great fighters tend to see the past as being better than the present. Wales produced very important boxers after Jimmy Wilde, but there were few who gained the world exposure and success he did. One cannot compare him as he went down the line, defeating flyweights, bantams, featherweights, and occasionally lightweights. There were, and still are, Welshmen who think Jimmy

Wilde could have beaten Jack Dempsey, Joe Louis and Muhammed Ali! The Prince of Wales certainly put Wilde on a pedestal. Of all the boxers to emerge before the First World War, Freddy Welsh, Jim Driscoll, Jimmy Wilde and Percy Jones contributed most to the reputation of Wales as a boxing nation, and stamped Britain's mark on world boxing. Jimmy Wilde's greatest asset was his brain, which was superior to the average professional boxer. Wilde could have become a celebrity as a golfer as well as a billiards player, but he chose boxing.

CHAPTER 17

SAD FAREWELL TO THE MIGHTY ATOM

Jimmy Wilde's life after his boxing days was something of an anticlimax, even though he achieved a great deal of good in his charity work. He never achieved stardom as a referee, even if he did travel far and wide to do the important work. The standards of refereeing in Britain are jealously guarded by the Referees' Association, and any prospective referee has to pass a strict examination, both written and practical, which Jimmy did. Refereeing by the twenties had become a fine art, and the excellent referee is respected.

A boxer who did become a famous referee was Jack Dempsey. In fact, Dempsey was one of the highest-paid referees ever in charge of a contest and, on two occasions, his fee plus expenses reached ten thousand dollars. Another outstanding referee was Eugene Corri, a stockbroker who refereed over one thousand contests in over fifty years. Most of these contests were held at The Ring, Blackfriars, London, where he was a huge favourite with the boxing fans during the period around World War One. Eugene Corri ended his refereeing career with a world title fight on 30 June 1927, when he was the third man in the ring for the middleweight bout between Mickey Walker and Tommy Milligan. Corri wrote extensively on Jimmy Wilde in Fifty Years in the Ring (London, 1933), a boxing classic. Wilde's fight with Alf Mansfield at the Holborn Stadium in 1919 was refereed by Corri. Wilde weighed in at six stone twelve pounds, his opponent being eight stone four pounds. Twenty pounds is a huge handicap, but as Corri said:

Jimmy Wilde not only won, but gave the doughty Mansfield so severe a thrashing that I had to stop the fight in the thirteenth round to save the loser further punishment.

Corri was amazed at Jimmy's speed, the force of his punches, and his timing, which he regarded as being part of his secret. Corri reminds us:

Add to these accomplishments his astonishing speed, his courage, and his flashes of unorthodoxy – often, for instance, he would leap fiercely at an opponent with both feet on the ground – and you will have some idea of the unsurpassed fighting machine called Jimmy Wilde.

It was Eugene Corri who refereed Wilde's fight with Pal Moore at Olympia in 1919, a contest watched by twenty thousand spectators.

The referee regarded Moore as a boxer who retained a bad habit for he often hit with an open glove. In the second round, Wilde had to face two stinging slaps in this fashion, and Corri cautioned him. When he did it in the third round, Corri warned him that if he did it again, he would be sent back to America with disqualification. Corri warned Moore again in the tenth round, but he realised that Wilde was gaining ground on points. In the thirteenth round, Moore rushed in and landed severe blows, which drew blood from the Welshman's mouth. In the sixteenth round, Moore, with a punch, accidentally butted Wilde in the nose, cutting the bridge to the bone.

Wilde was hurt and weakened, and he defended himself without his usual aggressiveness. He was determined to soldier on; however, he looked a sorry sight. The final round was thrilling, and twenty thousand people egged him on, but he was unable to deliver the knockout. The gong went. Corri ruled that Wilde had won on points. After his verdict was announced, the Welsh took over the ring. Wilde was mobbed. Hats, sticks, even chairs were flung into the air, and the Welsh choir raised their voices in song.

Eugene Corri saw Wilde as a marvelous boxer, and he soon organised an exhibition bout between the Tylorstown Terror and Bombardier Billy Wells. It was a three-round contest between the flyweight and the heavyweight, and owing to Wilde's agility and ability, Wells could not land a single punch. At last, he picked Wilde up and dropped him over the ropes. 'You worry me like a wasp!' he laughed, and so did the spectators. It was a perfect description of Wilde's boxing style. Corri describes Wilde losing to Tancy Lee back in 1915, and he recalls:

> I do not think I ever saw members of the NSC betray more sorrow over a man's defeat than they showed on that occasion. Even Tancy Lee himself seemed to be as much concerned about the little Welshman as elated by the victory.

Wilde came back, and a year later defeated Tancy Lee. Corri was present as a spectator when he fought Pete Herman, the famous American bantamweight, and lost after a hard belter of a contest. Corri recalls:

> So moved were some ringside spectators that they were actually in tears. Others had already left the hall, preferring to miss the rest of the fight rather than stay to watch the gallant little Wilde defeated.

Of Jimmy Wilde's last battle in New York against Pancho Villa, Corri believed the boxer had 'passed his zenith'. Sadly, Jimmy was never as successful outside the boxing ring as he was in it. In fact, he was never the same after the cruel battering he received from Pancho Villa in 1923. He was involved in a number of car accidents over a thirty-year period, the worst taking place at Dinas Powys in 1957 when Jimmy was on his way home to Cadoxton, Barry.

The incident accelerated his physical and mental decline. By 1960, symptoms of Alzheimer's disease had become apparent to his wife and sons.

Later that year, Jimmy was attacked on the platform at Queen Street railway station, Cardiff, while he was waiting for a train to Barry Island, where he owned a café. Had the forty-year-old Trethomas thug with a prison record tried it on with Wilde twenty years previously, he would have been knocked unconscious in no time. Describing the attack, Peter McInnes writes that Jimmy Wilde was 'butted in the face and kicked by creatures unfit to have washed his jock-strap in the good days'.

By 1965, Jimmy Wilde was in the grip of senile dementia and was admitted to Whitchurch Hospital. He also suffered from diabetes. Gareth Williams has described Wilde's dementia as proof 'that no sport compares with boxing in terms of the damage it does to the brain'. These days, more is understood about the danger of repeated concussion and constant blows to the head, and this has led to calls to reform the rules governing boxing.

In his article on Wilde, Gareth Williams makes a strong case for such reform:

> A knockout punch, medical experts tell us, can detach the skull from the brain within it, and damage the veins that connect the one to the other. Punch-drunkenness means the lessening of mental and physical capacities that results from long-term effects of repeated blows to the head. Jimmy Wilde was among the supermen of boxing and his life had sad ending. He suffered for his sport, despite giving thousands upon thousands of fans so much entertainment and pleasure by his skill.

Jimmy's beloved wife Elizabeth, or Lisabeth as he always called her, died in 1967. By then, his dementia had progressed too far for him to remember his glorious past when his wife had been his number one fan. Her love and support had been absolutely essential to him throughout his boxing career. For Elizabeth, there was nobody like 'our Jim'.

Jimmy died on 10 March 1969. Four days later, he was laid to rest in Barry cemetery next to Elizabeth. There was no sign of the thousands who had lined the route for Jimmy Driscoll's funeral in 1925.

In the annals of boxing, however, Jimmy Wilde's name will never be forgotten. He had the longest reign of any flyweight champion of the world, holding the title from 14 February 1916 to 18 June 1923, an impressive seven years and four months. Only three boxers have held a world championship longer than Jimmy Wilde: heavyweight Joe Louis (thirteen years and ninety-seven days), middleweight Tommy Ryan (eight years and eleven months) and the lightweight Irish-American Jack McAuliffe, nicknamed the Napoleon of the Ring (ten years).

In boxing history Jimmy Wilde is in good company, for he belonged to the glory days of Jim Driscoll and Freddie Welsh. Since that era, boxers like Tommy Farr, Howard Winstone, Dai Dower and Eddie Thomas have kept boxing in the news in south Wales. By 2008, Wales was again attracting publicity, with the success of Joe Calzaghe, the successful super middleweight and light heavyweight. As Eugene Corri said:

> Always in boxing, it is the heavyweight who draws the biggest crowds, receives the biggest purses, and generally wins the biggest share of the ephemeral fame of the Ring. That little fellow, though he may be – and usually is – twice as clever a boxer, had to be content with the scraps from the giant's table.

The exception was Jimmy Wilde. In Wales, he and Calzaghe top the league of the twentieth century's best boxers. That a referee of Eugene Corri's calibre awarded him the honorary title of 'the most amazing boxer' speaks volumes. During his long refereeing career (1880–1935), Corri saw Wilde in action many times. In his book *Welsh Warriors* (1990), Fred Deakin wrote, 'Wilde was the greatest flyweight who ever lived.' Thirty-one years later, his verdict still rings true.

BIBLIOGRAPHY

Bettinson, A. F., and Bennison B., The Home of Boxing (London: Odhams Press Limited, no date).

Carpentier, Georges, *My Fighting Life* (London: Cassell and Company Limited, 1920).

Golesworthy, Maurice (compiled), Encyclopedia of Boxing

(London: Robert Hale Limited, 1960).

Corri, Gene, *Fifty Years in the Ring* (London: Hutchinson and Co., 1933).

Gutteridge, Reg (Seconded by Henry Cooper), *The Big Punchers*

(rev. ed., London: Century Hutchinson, 1989).

Deakin, Fred, *Welsh Warriors* (Stone, Staffs.: Crescendo Publications, 1990).

Harris, Gareth, *Jimmy Wilde: World Champion Flyweight Boxer – Tylorstown Legend* (Cardiff: Coalopolis Publishing, 2006).

O'Leary, Paul, '"Peerless": The Life and Legend of Jim Driscoll', in Peter Stead and Gareth Williams (eds), *Wales and its Boxers: The Fighting Tradition* (Cardiff: University of Wales Press, 2008),17–31.

Palmer, Joe, Recollections of a Boxing Referee (London: John Lane the Bodley Head Ltd, 1927).

Smith, Dai, 'Freddie Welsh: Welsh American', in Peter Stead and Gareth Williams (eds), *Wales and its Boxers: The Fighting Tradition* (Cardiff: University of Wales Press, 2008), 33–53.

Stead, Peter, 'Hero of the Darkest Years: Jack Petersen', in Peter Stead and Gareth Williams (eds), *Wales and its Boxers*:

The Fighting Tradition (Cardiff: University of Wales Press, 2008), 71–86.

Williams, Gareth, '"A Brutal Passion": Bare-knuckle Bruisers and Mountain Fighters', in Peter Stead and Gareth Williams (eds), *Wales and its Boxers: The Fighting Tradition* (Cardiff: University of Wales Press, 2008), 3–16.

Williams, Gareth, 'Jimmy Wilde: the "Tylorstown Terror"', in Peter Stead and Gareth Williams (eds), *Wales and its Boxers: The Fighting Tradition* (Cardiff: University of Wales Press, 2008), 55–70.

ACKNOWLEDGEMENTS

Many a boxing commentator and author have been an inspiration, especially Gilbert Odd (1902–96), who served in his prime as editor of Boxing News and was, in my opinion, the best boxing historian in Britain. Odd served as a member of the British Board of Control from 1961 to 1969. He wrote to me here in Liverpool many years ago to inform me that I should write a book on Jimmy Wilde as well as another on the Rhondda boxer Tommy Farr. During the Covid-19 pandemic, I came across the research notes I had prepared in the mid-seventies for the book about Jimmy Wilde that Gilbert had suggested. The unprecedented events of 2020 gave me time to prepare the Jimmy Wilde story, as well as time to reflect on the style of a historian of the calibre of Gilbert Odd. Thanks are due to my colleague the Reverend Robert Parry, who typed the manuscript for publication, to David Fletcher, who brought the chapters together and took care of the photographs, and Dr. Pat Williams, who was at hand to read the manuscript as well as the proofs. I am very indebted to the Welsh Book Council and in particular the Editorial Department and the co-operation of Huw Meirion Edwards. I am most grateful to all four for their assistance. I did not have to bother anyone in a county archive or a library, and fortunately Boxing News was there to give a helping hand. I am delighted that Work Book of Las Vegas, USA will publish the book and that Calvin Richards and Heather Young have been so supportive on behalf of the publishers.

D. Ben Rees

APPENDIX

1 MORE ON WILDE

Black Friars, The Ring

For at least thirty years, The Ring was one of the most popular boxing arenas in London. A peculiar octagonal building situated in Blackfriars Road, it was originally a Nonconformist chapel which became redundant and was taken over by the former lightweight champion Dick Burge and his partner Tom Pritchard in 1910. Tragically, Burge died during World War One; however, his widow carried on her husband's work for another twenty-two years. She was the only female boxing promoter in Britain. The building was destroyed by German bombs during the Second World War, although not before great boxers of the calibre of Jimmy Wilde, Ted 'Kid' Lewis, Primo Carnera, Joe Beckett and many others had appeared in its ring.

Booths

The article by Gareth Williams is the best piece of writing on the boxing booths, which provided first-class preparation for those with a passion for boxing. Men like Jimmy Wilde, Jim Driscoll, Joe Beckett and Freddie Mills are among those who owed a huge debt to the experience they obtained in the old fairground boxing booths. I remember a boxing booth associated with the fair when it came to Aberystwyth.

British champions: Wilde as a titleholder in the flyweight division

1. Jimmy Wilde beat Symonds, pts 15, NSC, London, 16

November 1914. This was a non-title fight.

2. Tancy Lee beat Wilde, RSF, 17, NSC, London, 25 January 1915.
3. Jimmy Wilde beat Symonds, RSF, 12, NSC, London, 14 February 1916. Wilde relinquished the title in 1923.

Most contests in career

Without doubt, there were three in the top league. First, Bobby Dobbs, an African American who was born into slavery in Knoxville, Tennessee. Dobbs began fighting at 17 and didn't give it up until he was 56. During those thirty-nine years, he fought over a thousand bouts, including exhibitions. Jimmy Wilde comes second, claiming a total of 864 bouts, including those he fought in fairground booths. Most record books disagree with Wilde. They credit him with 138 bouts, but they leave out his boxing victories in the booths. Third is Sam Langford, the African Canadian who fought all weights from welter to heavy and is reckoned to have had 640 contests from the age of 15 until he retired at the age of 43. Len Harvey should also be mentioned here, fighting 418 contests during his twenty-three years in the ring.

Holborn Stadium, London

Built by promoter Jack Callaghan, the first contest staged at Holborn Stadium was for the world flyweight championship, when Jimmy Wilde beat Zulu Kid in eleven rounds on 18 December 1916. Another Welshman, Jack Peterson, won the British light heavyweight title from Harry Crossley in 1932 at Holborn Stadium.

Most knockouts

The record for a Welsh or British fighter is held by Jimmy Wilde. He scored sixty-seven knockouts from 1910 to 1923, but this high score does not include the many more knockouts he scored when fighting in fairground booths in Aberdare, Tonypandy and Tylorstown.

Liverpool Stadium

A popular centre for boxing since 1911, Liverpool Stadium became known as the Graveyard of Champions. On the other hand, many others made their reputation at Liverpool, local men like Nel Tarleton and Ernie Roderick. But the boxer who became a firm favourite in a city which had more Welsh people as inhabitants than any other city in England was Jimmy Wilde. He fought several of his earlier contests in Liverpool, venturing outside his home patch of Pontypridd, Cardiff and Tonypandy.

Lord Lonsdale belts

The first of these belts was presented to the National Sporting Club by the 5th Earl of Lonsdale in 1909. Among those who gained a Lonsdale belt in the early period were Tom T homas and Freddie Welsh in 1909, and Jim Driscoll in 1910. The remaining belts subsequently taken out of circulation by Wilde (flyweight), Johnny Basham (welterweight) and Pat O'Keefe (middleweight).

Lynch, Joe

Lynch had three fights in London between 1918 and 1919. Known as the Californian Peach, this Irish American reached the top of his class and became the world bantamweight champion in December 1920. He was less successful in London.

National Sporting Club, London

This exclusive club, which opened at 43 King Street, Covent Garden, on 5 March 1891, was a huge influence on boxing, not only in Britain, but internationally. It was founded by John Fleming and A. F. 'Peggy' Bettinson as a middle-class sporting club, and the Earl of Lonsdale was its first president. Jimmy Wilde and

Ted Lewis wanted Jimmy to box at the NSC; however, 'Peggy' Bettinson had to be convinced before the boxer was given a chance. Two contests, which took place after dinner before approximately 1,300 members and guests, were fought in total silence, for no talking was permitted within the building. Neither were women permitted in the audience, a rule which was broken by Elizabeth Wilde. After a long battle, Jimmy was eventually allowed to fight at the NSC and he made a huge impact. So much so, that when the club arranged a benefit night for Bettison in January 1914, Jimmy Wilde was invited to show his talent in the company of his mentor Jim Driscoll, Ted 'Kid' Lewis, Digger Stanley, Sam Langford, Billy Wells, Georges Carpentier and Kid McCoy. The NSC went into voluntary liquidation towards the end of 1940.

Ring magazine

Reg Gutteridge wrote in 1983:

> Incredible Wilde – tagged the Ghost with a Hammer in his Hands, the Tylorstown Terror – is the only non-American to be rated No.1 in the all-time greats list of Ring magazine.
>
> He was entered in the American Hall of Fame in 1959, forty-seven years after his final fight. American boxing men do not award an accolade to a Fancy Dan: they cherish a puncher.

Royalty and Jimmy Wilde

Members of the royal family have taken a great deal of interest in boxing since the days of King George I (1714–27). George IV formed a bodyguard of pugilists to attend his coronation ceremony at Westminster Abbey, which included John Jackson, Tom Belcher, Tom Cribb and Tom Spring. Of the royal family, it must have been Edward VIII (later the Duke of Windsor) and Albert (later King George VI) who were invited to the National Sporting Club more than anyone. Their grandfather, Edward VII, was introduced to John L. Sullivan while he was still Prince of Wales. In fact, the Prince of Wales had a close friendship with Jimmy Wilde. On 31 March 1919, he saw Jimmy outpoint Joe Lynch at the NSC. Two years later, on 13 January 1921, Edward climbed into the ring at the Albert Hall after Wilde's disputed fight with Joe Lynch to congratulate both men and soothe the crowd.

Symonds, Joe

Symonds, who hailed from Plymouth, was a hard-hitting flyweight who knocked out Percy Jones, the Welsh star from the Rhondda, but lost his title to Jimmy Wilde, who in turn knocked him out in twelve rounds at the NSC in February 1916. Symonds died at Plymouth in 1953 aged 59.

Villa, Pancho

The small, powerful Filipino became world flyweight champion when he knocked out the great Jimmy Wilde in the seventh round in New York on 18 June 1923. He had lost the American title to Frankie Genaro three months before he defeated Wilde. Villa defended his world title only once before he died in 1925 of blood poisoning following a tooth infection. This was a cause of sadness to Wilde and the boxing fraternity.

Lightest men to box professionally

Jimmy Wilde is on his own here. He is the lightest man ever to have taken part in first-class boxing, his fighting weight being just six stone and twelve pounds (96 pounds). Next to him would be Pascual Pérez of Argentina, who weighed in at a mere seven stone and eight pounds (106 pounds).

Longest reign as world champion

The longest reign as world champion in the flyweight division belongs to Jimmy Wilde. He held the title from 14 February 1916 to 18 June 1923 – a total of seven years and four months.

APPENDIX 2
Career record compiled by The Ring and Boxing News

Jimmy Wilde

Born 12 May 1892, Quaker's Yard near Edwardsville, Glamorganshire. Brought up in Pont-y-gwaith, Rhondda Fach, and fought as a boxer from Tylorstown. Died at Whitchurch Hospital, Cardiff, on March 10, 1969.

Abbreviations

D – drew

Dis – disqualified

DNC – declared no contest Exh – exhibition

KO – knockout L – lost

LF – lost on foul ND – no decision

Pts – points

RSF – referee stopped fight Rtd – retired

W – won

WD – won on disqualification WF – won on foul

YEAR OPPONENT LOCATION DECISION /ROUNDS

1911

18 Feb George Lake Pontypridd D 6

1911-1912

Lewis Williams	W. KO 3
Dick Jenkins	W. Pts 6
Fred Chappell	W. Pts 6
S. Jenkins Pontypridd	W. RSF 11
Jim Easton Edinburgh	W. Pts 10
Young Baker	W. Pts 6
Frank Avent	W. KO 3
Ted Powell	W. KO 3
Joe Rogers	W. KO 5
Kid Pearson	W. KO 7
Joe Gans	W. KO 5
Lewis Williams	W. KO 5
Mike Flynn	W. KO 8
Young Powell	W. KO 3
Ted Roberts	W. KO 3
Dai Roberts	W. KO 3
Young Langford	W. KO 2
Eddie Thomas	W. KO 2
Steve Thomas	W. KO 3
Billy Papke	W. KO 3
Archie Grant	W. KO 2
Young Towell	W. KO 4
Young Rice	W. KO 3
Walter Hall	W. RSF 3
Harry Stuckey	W. KO 7

1912

20 Jan	Matt Wells' Nipper Blackfriars	W. KO 1
20 July	Kid Morris Cardiff	W. Rtd 5
17 Aug	Jim Stuckey Tonypandy	W. Rsf 8
9 Nov	Phil Davie	W. Rtd 2
16 Nov	Young Ransford Tonypandy	W. Pts 2
30 Nov	Alf Williams Tonypandy	W. Pts 12
14 Dec	Stocker Staines Tonypandy	W. KO 1
21 Dec	Billy Yates Cardiff	W. Rtd 4
31 Dec	Billy Padden Glasgow	W. Rtd.18

1913

18 Jan	Tommy Hughes Tonypandy	W. KO 7
1 Feb	Dicky Jenkins Tonypandy	D 7
15 Feb	Kid Fitzpatrick Tonypandy	W. KO 2
Feb	Harry Stuckey Tonypandy	ND
Feb	Ben Hardwick Tylorstown	ND
8 Mar	Dai Matthews Tonypandy	W. KO 8
Mar	Harry Taylor Swansea	W. KO 3
12 April	Will Rees Tonypandy	W. KO 2
19 April	Bill Rees Tonypandy	W. KO 2
24 May	Dai Davies Tonypandy	W. Pts 12
	Kid Levene Tonypandy	W. KO 12
	Harry Brooks Manchester	W. KO 8
	Harry Curley	W. KO 12
14 June	Billy Padden Tonypandy	W. Pts 15
21 June	Gwilym Thomas Tonypandy	W. Rsf 5

1 July	Dick Lewis Tonypandy	W. Rtd 3
12 July	Tommy Lewis Tonypandy	W. Pts 12
19 July	Young Dando Tonypandy	W. Pts 15
4 Aug	Darkie Saunders Cardiff	W. Pts 10
28 Aug	Young Dyer Liverpool	W. Rsf 3
6 Sept	Dick Jenkins Ferndale	W. Rtd 10
8 Sept	Kid Lewis Hanley	W. Rtd 7
22 Sept	Young Dando Cardiff	W. Pts 20
1 Nov	Darkie Saunders Tonypandy	W. Rsf 11
13 Nov	Young Baker Liverpool	W. Rtd 10
21 Nov	Young Dyer Manchester	W. Rtd 10
22 Nov	Dado Gains Manchester	W. Rtd 15
6 Dec	Young Dando Merthyr	W.Dis 10
13 Dec	Billy Charles Tonypandy	W. Rtd 6

1914

3 Jan	Kid Nutter Tonypandy	W. Pts 15
8 Jan	Young Beynon Liverpool	W.Pts 15
29 Jan	Harry Paddon Liverpool	W. Rtd 5
2 Feb	Kid Nutter Birkenhead	W. Pts 15
9 Feb	Tom Thomas Manchester	W. KO 7
12 Feb	Paddy Carroll Liverpool	W. KO 2
16 Feb	George Jaggers Sheffield	W. Rsf 5
26 Mar	Bill Kyne Liverpool	W. Rsf 4
13 April	Eugene Husson London (NSC)	W.KO 6
16 April	Jack Madden Ashton under Lyne	W.KO 4
27 April	Alf Mansfield Leeds	W. Pts 20
11 May	George GloriaNSC	W. Rsf 9
22 June	Charles Banyard Aberdare	W.Rsf 10

18 July	Charley Jordan Tonypandy	W. Rsf 10
23 July	Artie Edwards Liverpool	W.Pts 15
19 Aug	Young Baker Leicester	W. Pts 15
28 Sept	Alf Mansfield West London Stadium	W. Rtd 10
16 Nov	Joe Symonds NSC	W. Pts 15

(British flyweight title eliminator)

3 Dec	Sid Smith Liverpool	W. Rsf 8

1915

25 Jan	Tancy Lee NSC	L. Rtd 17

(British and European flyweight title and Lonsdale belt)

25 Mar	Sid Shields Liverpool	W. KO 2
24 July	Driver Benthew Sheffield	W.Rtd 5
14 Aug	George Clarke Sheffield	W.Rtd 8
23 Sept	Walter Buchan Liverpool	W.Rtd 5
20 Oct	Tommy Hughes Barrow	W.Rtd 8
27 Nov	Tommy Hughes Barrow	W. Rtd 8
9 Dec	Johnny Best Liverpool	W.Rsf1 4
16 Dec	Danny Elliot Bradford	W.KO 2
20 Dec	Sid Smith Liverpool	W. Rsf 8
8 Jan	Billy Rowlands 1916 Swansea	W. Rsf 7
24 Jan	Tommy Noble New Cross	W. Rtd 11
27 Jan	Jimmy Morton Liverpool	W. KO 2
14 Feb	Joe Symonds NSC	W. Rtd 11

(British and European flyweight title and Lonsdale belt)

9 Mar	Sam Keller West London Stadium	W.Rtd 8
24 April	Johnny Rosner Liverpool	W.Rtd 11

(world flyweight title)

29 April	Benny Thomas Cardiff	W.Pts	8
13 May	Darkey Saunders Woolwich	W. Rsf	3
13 May	Young Magnus Woolwich	W. KO	2
29 May	Tommy Harrison Oxford Music Hall	W.Rtd	8
26 June	Tancy Lee NSC	W.Rsf	11

(British and European flyweight title and Lonsdale belt)

31 July	Johnny Hughes Kensal Rise	W. KO	9
Nov	Tommy Noble Liver pool	W. Rsf	15
18 Dec	Young Zulu Kid Holborn	W.KO	11

(world flyweight title)

1917

12 Mar	George Clarke NSC	W. Rtd	4

(British and European flyweight title and Lonsdale belt outright)

22 Mar	Frankie Russell Holborn	W. Rsf	3

1918

28 Mar	L/Cpl Jacobs Aldershot	W.Rsf	4
29 April	Dick Heasman NSC	W. Rtd	2
31 Aug	Joe Conn Stamford Bridge	W. Rsf	12
11 Dec	PTE Joe Lynch Albert Hall	W. Pts	3
11 Dec	Digger Evans Albert Hall	W. Pts	3
12 Dec	Pal Moore Albert Hall	L. Pts	3

(final of bantamweight class of ISBA King's Trophy Competition)

1919

31 Mar	Joe Lynch NSC	W. Pts 15
21 April	Jimmy Buck Liverpool	W. KO 5
16 May	Alf Mansfield Holborn	W.Rsf 13
17 July	Pal Moore Olympia	W. Pts 20
6 Dec	Jack Sharkey Milwaukee	ND 10

1920

8 Jan	Babe Asher St Louis	ND 8
29 Jan	Mike Ertle Milwaukee	W.KO 3
15 Feb	Mickey Russell Jersey City	W KO 7
3 Mar	Patsy Wallace Philadelphia	ND 6
12 Mar	Frankie Mason Toledo	ND 12
12 April	Zulu Kid Windsor, Ontario	ND 10
21 April	Battling Murray Camden, New Jersey	W.KO8
1 May	Bobby Dyson Lawrence	W. KO 1
13 May	Battling Murray Philadelphia	W. KO 2
24 May	Patsy Wallace Toronto	W. Pts 10

1921

| 13 Jan | Pete Heasman Albert Hall | L. Rsf 17 |

1923

| 18 June | Pancho Villa New York | L. KO 7 |

(world flyweight title)

APPENDIX 3

WHAT THEY SAID ABOUT JIMMY WILDE

'None comparable to Jimmy Wilde,' Georges Carpentier (champion heavyweight boxer of Europe) wrote in *My Fighting Life*.

None of us will ever see the like of him again. As a boxer, he is an outrage on convention. Wilde belongs to no school: he is all wrong, and yet supreme. For he is a human shadow. Physically of not much account, he is yet a man of steel. This is the perspective I would draw of this uncanny Welshman:

> Baby-faced, with grey, dull, sleepy, little eyes; hair thin; neck skinny; arms like yard sticks; feet, for his size, inordinately big, almost flat-footed. The first time I beheld him, it was impossible for me to believe that he was the most wonderful fighter in the world. Yet he was …

Then he wrote:

> Maybe Wilde has had his greatest day, but as long as the ring lasts, we shall surely remember him as a pugilistic marvel, a speck of a man – only just a trifle more than seven stones were he when at his best – who was a versatile giant-killer. Wilde, from the first day he wandered from the South Wales coalfields, was the David of the ring, and he slew not one, but many Goliaths.

F. Bettinson and B. Bennison write in The Home of Boxing about Jimmy Wilde:

When we come to discuss the flyweights, we must begin and stop with Jimmy Wilde. He is incomparable. We hailed Sid Smith as an unusual little man in 1911; we thought ever so highly of Percy Jones; we have already praised Tancy Lee – but Jimmy Wilde stands alone. Before he went to America, he could give stones away and win in a canter. Of this wonderful, strange, uncanny Welshman, it is impossible to employ words to express our admiration; we can only say that his name will endure for all time.

Joe Lynch, the marvelous boxer from the USA, lost in three rounds in the Services Tournament to Wilde. Jimmy Wilde, in tackling Lynch, one of the best of all bantams, achieved an incredible performance. It was a great contest, and Lynch said at the end:

> It is my proud privilege to have fought at your National Sporting Club, and to have met such a marvelous boxer as Wilde. You will agree that it was a hard fight. With my showing, I am thoroughly satisfied.

Gareth Williams describes Jimmy Wilde in all his brilliance and, in particular, his stinging left, which he compares to a piston rod. He goes on to say:

> Wilde could hit very hard and very fast with both. Not for nothing does Ring magazine rank him third in its list of the hundred greatest all-time punchers, behind only Joe Louis and Sam Langford. Though past his prime by the time he visited the USA in 1919–1920, in Philadelphia in his second fight with Battling Murray, a right to the jaw lifted Murray off his feet, and bounced him off the ropes back on to the canvas.

Reg Gutteridge, the journalist and TV commentator, in a chapter on Wilde in his bestseller The Big Punchers, mentions how the boxing promoter Jack Solomons invited Jimmy Wilde into the ring to be introduced to the crowd in the late 1950s. Gutteridge writes:

> Then Wilde grabbed the microphone and, while pointing to the champion and the challenger announced: 'I'd beat the

> pair of them'. He was in his sixties. The crowd laughed, the boxers blushed and the promoter was angry.

> It was the last time Jimmy was publicly introduced. He reckoned the flyweights of the sixties were 'bloody slow'. In the history of the British flyweight division, only Lynch and perhaps another Scot, Jackie Paterson, could match Wilde's freakish punch power.

> Henry Cooper, one of Britain's most admired boxers, said: The speed of Wilde's punches would be bewildering to me. He had the ingredients of being fearless, which made him able to wade in and hit where it hurts. The little fellow was a one-off. He must have been marvelous for the Americans to rate him the best at 8 stone.

Hywel Teifi Edwards, in his scintillating article '"Boxing Mad" in Cardi-land, 1945–1955', in Wales and its Boxers, writes about Jimmy Wilde:

Jimmy Wilde held the world flyweight title from 1916 to 1923, and in the words of R. A. Haldane, was 'the greatest pugilist of any weight and on any day since glove-fighting began, that country ever produced'. For a Bethel frequenting school boy, that was a tribute of Old Testament proportions.

Baptised 'The Ghost with a Hammer in his Hand' by Pedlar Palmer, the former world bantamweight title holder, this potent Rhondda-born sprite could have emerged from some Celtic netherworld to undo mere mortals, so extraordinary was the power his gaming physique could generate. It takes some believing that he could weigh in for a world flyweight contest at eight stones 'fully-clothed, with overcoat and bowler hat on, and carrying his hand-case', and still make the weight comfortably. During the Great War (surely to the Kaiser's relief) he could not serve at the front 'because he weighed less than the regulation Army pack'.

APPENDIX 4

GREATEST BOXERS OF ALL TIME

In December 2000, Kevin Mitchell, The Observer's chief sportswriter, nominated ten greatest boxers of all time as follows:

1. Muhammad Ali
2. Sugar Ray Robinson
3. Joe Louis
4. Jimmy Wilde
5. Benny Leonard
6. Archie Moore
7. Jack Johnson
8. Sugar Ray Leonard
9. Jack Dempsey
10. Henry Armstrong

Many responded to his list. John Davies of Brecon, Powys, had the following on his list:

1. Sugar Ray Robinson
2. Jack Johnson
3. Muhammad Ali
4. Joe Gans
5. Roberto Duran
6. Joe Lewis
7. Jimmy Wilde
8. George Dixon
9. Daniel Mendoza

Reader Gareth Welch felt that Jimmy Wilde was a true great who has been 'shamefully neglected in Britain'.

Keith Simons broadly agreed with Mitchell's list, but would include Roberto Duran, who he called 'the greatest of the lightweights' and who he thought should replace Jack Dempsey at number nine.

Gerald Suster, a reader of The Observer and author of Champions of the Ring: The Lives and Times of Boxing's Heavyweight Heroes, placed Jimmy Wilde in ninth position:

1. Muhammad Ali
2. Sugar Ray Robinson
3. J. Johnson
4. Joe Louis
5. Willie Pep
6. Carlos Monzon
7. Manuel Octiz
8. Joe Gans
9. Jimmy Wilde
10. Archie Moore

Another reader, responded with a list which also puts Jimmy Wilde at number nine:

1. Sugar Ray Robinson
2. Muhammad Ali
3. Henry Armstrong
4. Archie Moore
5. Jack Johnson
6. Benny Leonard

7. Sugar Ray Leonard

8. Julio Cesar Chavez

9. Jimmy Wilde

10. Evander Holyfield

Ceri Kneath of Swansea omits Jimmy Wilde from the list entirely, with no explanation:

1. Roberto Duran

2. Mickey Walker

3. Sugar Ray Robinson

4. Muhammad Ali

5. Jack Johnson

6. Rocky Marciano

7. Carlos Monzon

8. Roy Jones

9. Joe Louis

10. Stanley Ketchel

APPENDIX 5

THE BEST BRITISH FLYWEIGHTS IN JIMMY WILDE'S BOXING CAREER

1913 champion: Bill Ladbury (Greenwich)
1. Percy Jones, Porth, Wales
2. Joe Symonds, Plymouth, England
3. Jimmy Wilde, Tylorstown, Wales
4. Tancy Lee, Paisley, Scotland
5. George Dando, Merthyr, Wales
6. Charlie Ward, Blackfriars, London
7. Johnny Best, Glasgow, Scotland
8. Harry Carley, Lambeth, London
9. Joe Wilson, Stepney, London
10. Alf Mansfield, Aldgate, London

1914 champion: Percy Jones (Porth)
1. Tancy Lee, Paisley, Scotland
2. Jimmy Wilde, Tylorstown, Wales
3. Bill Ladbury, Vauxhall, London
4. Joe Symonds, Plymouth, England
5. George Dando, Merthyr Wales
6. Johnny Best, Glasgow, Scotland
7. Dido Gains, Vauxhall, London

8. Charlie Ward, Blackfriars, London

9. Billy Rowlands, Porthcawl, Wales

10. Joe Wilson, Stepney, London

1915 champion: Joe Symonds (Plymouth)

1. Tancy Lee, Paisley, Scotland

2. Jimmy Wilde, Tylorstown, Rhondda, Wales

3. Bill Eynon, Merthyr, Wales

4. George Dando, Merthyr, Wales

5. Bill Ladbury, Greenwich, London

6. Dido Gains, Vauxhall, London

7. Ivor Day, Porth, Wales

8. George Clark, Bermondsey, London

9. Billy Rowlands, Porthcawl, Wales

10. Johnny Best, Glasgow, Scotland

1916 champion: Jimmy Wilde (Tylorstown)

1. George Clark, Bermondsey, London

2. Sid Smith, Bermondsey, London

3. Bill Eynon, Merthyr Tydfil, Wales

4. Bill Ladbury, Greenwich, London

5. Walter Ross, Glasgow, Scotland

6. Lewis Williams, Pen-y-graig, Rhondda, Wales

7. Dido Gains, Merthyr, Wales

8. Dick Sorris, Cardiff, Wales

9. Bill Rowlands, Porthcawl, Wales

10. Frankie Ash, Plymouth

1917 champion: Jimmy Wilde (Tylorstown)

1. Billy Eynon, Merthyr, Wales
2. Alf Mansfield, Aldgate, London
3. Arthur Bishop, Caerphilly, Wales
4. Lewis Williams, Pen-y-graig, Rhondda, Wales
5. Tal Jones, Maesteg, Wales
6. Frankie Ash, Plymouth, England
7. Billy Matthews, St James, London
8. Gus Legge, Abertillery, Wales
9. Ned Dixon, Porth, Wales
10. Dick Sorris, Cardiff, Wales

1918 champion: Jimmy Wilde (Tylorstown)

1. Lewis Williams, Pen-y-graig, Wales
2. Billy Eynon, Merthyr, Wales
3. Young Chips, Tylorstown, Wales
4. Arthur Bishop, Caerphilly, Wales
5. Tal Jones, Maesteg, Wales
6. Harold Jones, Ferndale, Wales
7. Frankie Ash, Plymouth, England
8. Dick Heasman, Southwark, London
9. Alf Mansfield, Aldersgate, London.
10. Jack Kid Doyle, Salford, England

1919 champion: Jimmy Wilde (Tylorstown)

1. Jack Kid Doyle, Salford, England
2. Lewis Williams, Pen-y-graig, Wales
3. Frankie Ash, Plymouth, England

4. Arthur Bishop, Caerphilly, Wales

5. George Langham, Clerkenwell, London

6. Dick Heasman Southwark, London

7. Alf Mansfield, Aldgate, London

8. Sammy Jones, Ystradgynlais, Wales

9. Johnny Broker, Marylebone, London

10. Tal Jones, Maesteg, Wales

1920 champion: Jimmy Wilde (Tylorstown)

1. Frankie Ash, Plymouth, England

2. Jack Kid Doyle, Salford, England

3. Bugler Harry Lake, Plymouth, England.

4. George Langham, Clerkenwell, London

5. Lewis Williams, Pen-y-graig, Wales

6. Gus Legge, Abertillery, Wales

7. Dick Heasman, Southwark, London

8. George Garrard, Acton, London

9. Sammy Jones, Ystradgynlais, Wales

10. Johnny Broker, Marylebone, London

1921 champion: Jimmy Wilde (Tylorstown)

1. Frankie Ash , Plymouth, England

2. Jack Kid Doyle, Salford, England

3. George Mapplebeck, West Melton, England

4. George Garrard, Acton, London

5. Bugler Harry Lake, Plymouth, England

6. Sammy Jones, Ystradgynlais, Wales

7. Jim Blackley, Edinburgh, Scotland

8. Billy Morris, Birkenhead, England

9. Kid Kelly, Plymouth, England

10. Harry Aarons, Brixton, London

1922 champion: Jimmy Wilde (Tylorstown)

1. Frankie Ash, Plymouth, England

2. Teddy Murton, Plymouth, England

3. George Garrard, Acton, London

4. Billy Morris, Birkenhead, England

5. George Mapplebeck, West Melton, England

6. Jim Blackley, Edinburgh, Scotland

7. Tal Jones, Maesteg, Wales

8. Kid Kelly, Plymouth, England

9. Johnny Jones, Treorchy, Wales

10. Johnny Broker, Marylebone, London

INDEX

Lightning Source UK Ltd.
Milton Keynes UK
UKHW022001120922
408762UK00008B/1927